THE CHILDREN'S BREAD

DELIVERANCE FROM MINDSETS &
STRONGHOLDS

TERRA KERN

Higher Ground Books & Media
HGBM

Scripture taken from the HOLY BIBLE, NEW INTERNATIONAL VERSION®. NIV®. Copyright © 1973, 1978, 1984 by International Bible Society. Used by permission of Zondervan. All rights reserved worldwide.

Higher Ground Books & Media
P.O. Box 2914
Springfield, OH 45501-2914
www.highergroundbooksandmedia.com

Because of the dynamic nature of the Internet, any web addresses or links contained in this book may have changed since publication and may no longer be valid. The views expressed in the work are solely those of the author and do not necessarily reflect the views of the publisher, and the publisher hereby disclaims any responsibility for them.

Any people depicted in stock imagery are being used for illustrative purposes only.

Printed in the United States of America 2024

THE CHILDREN'S BREAD

DELIVERANCE FROM MINDSETS & STRONGHOLDS

TERRA KERN

Foreword

Richard Nowik, Associate Pastor

Mt Zion, Clarkston, MI

In 1984 my parents began their search for the Lord and took all three of their sons with them on their journey. We will forever be indebted to parents willing to face family ridicule and even loss of relationship for leaving the traditional church for a personal relationship with Jesus Christ. From our church background there was no exposure to the things of the spirit or even the mystical things demonstrated in the charismatic / Pentecostal movement our parents were drawn to. As a teenager, I was mostly apprehensive and more often confused by the things I was seeing or hearing because I had no knowledge of the Word of God. During these early years of my own walk with the Lord I received the Holy Spirit into my life and started my walk with Christ. It was not always smooth. In fact, I am confident my mom was convinced, in those early years of my walk, I needed great deliverance on more than one occasion! These 40 years later, and as a minister for more than 25 years, I have learned so much about the Lord and have so much more to understand about the kingdom of God.

I know He is shining a light into areas we have only "understood in part" to bring greater clarity to the Body of Christ and one of those areas in need of addressing is deliverance. Through her other books and at the leading of the Lord, Terra Kern is reconciling the things she has learned over the years versus what the Lord is revealing to her as part of this present truth. I appreciate Terra's words in The Children's Bread: Deliverance from Mindsets and Strongholds confronting long held mindsets that have prevented the church from walking in maturity. Terra delves into the devil's strongholds and, through the Word of God, illuminates the real power available to us so we can walk in freedom and liberty. She boldly proclaims, "We need to shift our thinking from the mindset of fear and/or intimidation when we see the enemy at work, when we recognize the spirit of the world, the spirit of the age, powers, principalities, wickedness in high places, the wiles of the devil, the demonic, etc. to the mindset of seeing God at work..." It is time to take our eyes off the enemy and fix them on what God is doing!

In 2 Corinthians 10:4-5 we are instructed, "For the weapons of our warfare are not carnal but mighty in God for pulling down strongholds, casting down arguments and every high thing that exalts itself against the knowledge of God, <u>bringing every thought into captivity</u> to the obedience of Christ." (emphasis my own). The strength of our enemy is his lies and the power of his persuasions in a system he has created to enslave humanity. I am thankful for people like Terra who are willing to address the issues within the church and the mindsets we have embraced, so we can walk in a new level of understanding and maturity.

PREFACE

Way in the back of my mind, I heard a very still, small voice say, "I want you to write a book on deliverance." I stopped what I was doing and acknowledged hearing what was spoken, then pushed it aside as not being from God, asking myself, "What do I know about deliverance?" Now, let's fast-forward a few weeks later after prayer service. An intercessor prayed for me and said she heard the Lord saying He was calling me into a ministry of deliverance and was indeed giving me a double portion anointing for deliverance in this new season. Well, hmm... As I later pondered upon this, that same still, small voice spoke again repeating, "I want you to write a book on deliverance." Now, I am known for saying that you don't have to tell me twice, but I apparently can't say that here, for obviously, I had to be. But I am thankful that God is patient and that He gave me confirmation.

As I prayed and sought the Lord, the Holy Spirit began to open up the Scriptures. I was truly amazed at what He is bringing forth in this new day that is upon us. Scriptures that I have read before had new meaning as He brought focus to words or phrases in them that I had sort of skimmed over in the past, bringing revelation and correction within them. The Holy Spirit completely blew my mind so many times as He revealed His Word to me regarding deliverance, our minds, our brains, mindsets, strongholds, and our thoughts. Every single thing begins with a thought! As He brought back to my memory some scientific studies I had heard of and even my medical training on how our brains function, He revealed how science has been and still is confirming what His Word has said all along! God never ceases to amaze me!

The Bible truly is a living Word and I pray that all of what He has opened up to me in my understanding would be a blessing to you also, and that as you read this book and the revelations held within, that He would lead you into deliverance in ways you've not known or experienced before, and bring you into maturity in Him, all for His glory! I pray that He would be with you and lead you into all He has created you to be as He brings His church into unity, in the mighty name of Jesus! Amen!

John 6:48 – And Jesus said to them, "I am the bread of life."

Joel 2:32…For in Mount Zion and in Jerusalem there shall be deliverance, as the Lord has said, Among the remnant whom the Lord calls.

Hebrews 12:22-24 – But you have come to Mount Zion and to the city of the living God, the heavenly Jerusalem, to an innumerable company of angels, to the general assembly and church of the firstborn who are registered in heaven, to God the Judge of all, to the spirits of just men made perfect (mature) to Jesus the Mediator of the new covenant, and to the blood of sprinkling that speaks better things than that of Abel.

Revelation 18:10… Alas, alas that great city Babylon, that mighty city! For in one hour your judgment has come.

Revelation 18:20 – "Rejoice over her, O heaven, and you holy apostles and prophets, for God has avenged you on her!"

CHAPTER ONE

THE CHILDREN'S BREAD

We, the people of God, are living in great and exciting times as we have entered into a new season, a new visitation of God. Within this visitation, God is going to be bringing about marvelous and miraculous things. And in order for us to walk in these things, He first needs to bring His light of revelation and correction to the darkness of error that has been taught and acted upon in times past, just as He has been doing in other areas of His Word. Just as He has in the prior visitations and moves of God all throughout church history. As we are now in a new day, the third day, where our spiritual eyes will be opened to truths and mysteries here-to-fore hidden in the Word of God, it is pertinent that we seek Him in a much greater degree and make sure that we have ears to hear and eyes to see what the Spirit is speaking and teaching so that God can give us a greater Spiritual perception and bring us into maturity, into a bride without spot nor wrinkle nor any such thing, into a perfected and powerful people all moving in the unity of His Spirit. Or in other words, all of His people going forth being on the same page in particular areas of teachings, and doing so victoriously. One such area God is shining His light on and calling for unity and maturity in is in the arena of deliverance.

In both Matthew and Mark, we are taught that deliverance is the children's bread. Matthew 15:22-28 reads, And behold, a woman of Caanan came from that region of Tyre and cried out to Him, saying, "Have mercy on me, O Lord, Son of David! My daughter is severely demon possessed." But He answered her not a word. And His disciples came and urged Him, saying, "Send her away, for she cries out after us." But He answered and said, "I was not sent except to the lost sheep of the house of Israel." Then she came and worshipped Him, saying, "Lord, help me!" But He answered and said, "It is not good to take the children's bread and throw it to the dogs." And she said, "Yes Lord, yet even the little dogs eat the crumbs which fall from the masters' table." Then Jesus answered and said to her, "O woman, great is your faith! Let it be to you as you de-sire." And her daughter was healed from that very hour.

Mark gives us a little more information about the woman, emphasizing the fact that she was a Gentile and most certainly not from the house of Israel. Mark 7:25-30 says it this way – For a woman whose young daughter had an unclean spirit heard about Him, and she came and fell at His feet. The woman was a Greek, a Syro-Phoenician by birth, and she kept asking Him to cast the demon out of her daughter. But Jesus said to her, "Let the children be filled first, for it is not good to take the children's bread and throw it to the little dogs." And she answered and said to Him, "Yes Lord, yet even the little dogs under the table eat from the children's crumbs." Then He said to her, "For this saying go your way; the demon has gone out of your daughter." And when she had come to her house, she found the demon gone out, and her daughter lying on the bed.

There are two things I'd like to emphasize regarding the above-mentioned passages of Scripture. First off, Jesus delivered the woman's daughter from demonic possession due to the woman's faith. Jesus, the bread of life, was called to minister to Israel first, as it was their set time. Ecclesiastes 3:1 tells us there is a set time for everything. "To everything there is a season, a time for every purpose under heaven." There was a set time for the Gentiles to hear the good news of the gospel too, but this was not it. We know Gentiles would indeed be brought into Jesus' fold for way back in Genesis, God told Abraham that all of the nations of the world be blessed through his seed. Genesis 22:18 – "In your seed all the nations of the earth shall be blessed, because you have obeyed My voice" So all of the other nations beyond the nation of Israel would be blessed in their due time and season, but again, this was not that time. Jesus told the woman that now was not the time of the Gentiles' getting bread. But because the woman had heard about all of the miracles Jesus was performing, especially the casting out of demons, she recognized Him as the coming Messiah. We know this by her referring to Jesus as the son of David as prophesied about in Isaiah 9:6-7 "For unto us a Child is born, unto to us a Son is given; And the government shall be upon His shoulder. And His name will be called Wonderful, Counselor, Mighty God, Everlasting Father, Prince of Peace. Of the increase of His government and peace, there will be no end, upon the throne of David and over His kingdom, to order it and establish it with judgement and justice from that time forward, even forever. The zeal of the Lord will perform this." Therefore, she knew and believed that just a wee little crumb of His power could deliver her daughter. She then went on to let Him know that she wasn't asking for the whole loaf of bread that wasn't hers to partake of, just a wee little crumb to be dropped on the floor for her. She had that great of faith and Jesus honored it.

The second thing, and most pertinent relative to this book, is that the children's bread is deliverance. The very first time Jesus spoke in public in the synagogue, He said as much. We find this in Luke 4:18-19 when he quoted Isaiah 61:1-3, letting the people know He was there in fulfillment of that prophecy. The passage in Luke reads, "The Spirit of the Lord is upon me, Because He has anointed Me To preach the gospel to the poor; He has sent Me to heal the brokenhearted, To proclaim liberty to the captives And recovery of sight to the blind, To set at liberty those who are oppressed; To proclaim the acceptable year of the LORD." Jesus' decree to us, the children of God, is to deliver us from every oppression or captivity or anything and everything contrary to His Word that we are caught up in that threatens to do us harm and keep us from becoming all God has planned for us. The children's bread is deliverance.

2 Corinthians 1:9-10 says, Yes, we had the sentence of death in ourselves but in God who raises the dead, who delivered us from so great a death, and does deliver us; in whom we trust that He will still deliver us. 2 Timothy 4:17-18 reads, But the Lord stood with me and strengthened me, so that the message might be preached fully through me, and that all the Gentiles might hear. Also, I was delivered out of the mouth of the lion. And the Lord will deliver me from every evil work and preserve me for His heavenly kingdom. To Him be glory forever and ever. Amen! – Deliverance is the children's bread.

Psalm 91:14-16 – "Because he has set his love upon Me, therefore I will deliver him; I will set him on high, because he has known My name. He shall call upon Me, and I will answer him; I will be with him in trouble; I will deliver him and honor him. With long life I will satisfy him, And show him My salvation." Joel 2:32 proclaims – "And it shall come to pass That whoever calls on the name of the LORD shall be saved. For in Mount Zion and in Jerusalem there shall be deliverance, as the LORD has said, Among the remnant whom the Lord calls." Obadiah 1:17 – "But on Mount Zion there shall be deliverance, And there shall be holiness; The house of Jacob shall possess their possessions." God is the same yesterday, today and forever, so yes, deliverance is still the children's bread. Now that we have unequivocally determined that deliverance is the children's bread, let's focus on other aspects of deliverance.

In times past, the church, the ecclesia, the whole body of Christ, has done great damage to itself as well as to others around them in the arena of deliverance. It is true that God has equipped us with power from on high and has given us a very powerful, potent weapon. And that weapon is the Word of God, the sword of the Spirit. Hebrews 4:12 teaches us – "For the Word of God is living and powerful, and sharper than any two-edged sword, piercing even to the division of soul and spirit, and of joints and marrow, and is a discerner of the thoughts and intents of the heart." And Ephesians 6:17 tells us that it is actually a part of our whole armor of God that we are to put on and utilize. "And take the helmet of salvation, and the sword of the Spirit, which is the Word of God".

In the natural, it is a well-known fact that whoever has the most powerful weapon, wins the fight. Think of the numerous movies and even cartoons you've seen where combat is taking place between two fighters. In that scuffle, one fighter has his weapon jarred from his grip and it goes flying, landing a distance away. In that moment, both parties make eye contact, their gazes shift over to the loose weapon, then back to their foe, eyes locked upon one another again. And after that, in a split second, a mad dash toward that weapon is made by both of them. They know whoever has the most powerful weapon wins and also that if they are able to disarm the other from their weapon, their adversary then loses their power and they themselves will become the victor. It is exactly what Jesus did when he defeated all of the enemy. Colossians 2:15 reads – "Having dis-armed principalities and powers, He (Jesus) made a public spectacle of them, triumphing over them in it."

It also is true in the natural that in order for one to be proficient in wielding a weapon, they have to be properly trained in how to use the weapon or they could hurt themselves and/or others with it, and in fact, lose the fight. Let's take a gun for example. All too often we hear in the news lately where small children have found an unsecured gun and either shot themselves, or another child. They are severely injured and, in some cases, killed. Sometimes the child injures or kills themself and sometimes the child injures or kills another. In either case, whether severely injured or killed, damage has been done and it all comes down to having not been properly trained in how to use that powerful weapon. As well as them being young and immature, and not realizing what a powerful weapon they hold in their hands. In the same way, the Word of God and the power and authority Jesus gave to us, as well as us being endued with power from on high once we were baptized in the Holy Spirit, are very powerful weapons indeed! God has placed a very powerful weapon in our hands. And if not properly trained in how to wield our weapon, the sword of the Spirit, we can cause unintended damage too, as previously stated.

As an example, the Lord gave me the story of David battling the giant Goliath. David was just a youth when he volunteered to fight the giant when none of the warriors from the army would, due to their fear of Goliath. 1 Samuel 17 tells the story. When King Saul came to David after hearing what he had been saying, David said to Saul, "Let no man's heart fail because of him; your servant will go and fight with this Philistine." And Saul said to David, "You are not able to go against this Philistine to fight with him; for you are a youth and he a man of war from his youth." Then after David explained to Saul how he had taken out both bears and lions while watching over his father's flocks, he added, "The Lord who delivered me from the paw of the lion and from the paw of the bear, He will deliver me from the hand of this Philistine." Upon hearing this, Saul gave David his blessing, so to speak, and then clothed David in his armor which included his bronze helmet, his coat of mail, and his sword. But David couldn't even walk with them, yet alone fight with them. He wasn't accustomed to them, had not tested them, and had not been trained with them. So, at this point, David takes them off and gathers up the weapon he was accustomed to, his sling and stones. We all know the rest of the story. David defeats Goliath, taking him down with just that sling and a stone. We later see in the Scriptures that as David grows up and matures, he is a valiant and successful warrior wielding his sword and conquering enemy army after enemy army. We can see one example of this in 1 Samuel 18:7 – So the women sang as they danced, and said: "Saul has slain his thousands, And David his ten thousands."

What the Lord showed me in this, is that when David was a youth, immature if you will, he fought with the weapon he was familiar with, had tested, and been trained in, that sling and stone as opposed to a sword, a weapon that was too big for him to handle. Then as David grew and matured, he tested the sword and became trained in swordsmanship, learning the skills and techniques used in combat with a sword. If David had continued to Goliath with that sword, the outcome of the fight would have been much different. The Lord explained to me that is exactly what has happened in the church. Some ministers, not having been trained properly in the use of the sword of the Spirit, therefore being immature with it, tried to fight battles incorrectly with it and lost doing damage not only to themselves and others, but also to the reputation of the church as a whole. We'll delve into this in more depth later on.

See, God's desire for us, in this new season, is to come forth as a mighty army of God, surrounded by an innumerable angel army as we go forth as called, and tear down mindsets and strongholds, and bring deliverance to captives and as Ephesians 3:9-11 tells us – and to make all see what is the fellowship of the mystery, which from the beginning of the ages has been hidden in God who created all things through Jesus Christ; to the intent that now the manifold wisdom of God might be made known by the church to the principalities and powers in the heavenly places, according to the eternal purpose which He accomplished in Christ Jesus our Lord."

Paul tells us in 2 Corinthians 10:4-5 – "For the weapons of our warfare are not carnal but mighty in God for pulling down strongholds, casting down arguments and every high thing that exalts itself against the knowledge of God, bringing every thought into captivity to the obedience of Christ". From this Scripture, we learn that this warfare takes place in minds and thought processes. We'll discuss strongholds and mindsets in more depth in the next upcoming chapters, but for now let's just focus on the fact that a stronghold in the mind is a spiritual fortress made up of wrong thoughts and mindsets, high thoughts that exalt themselves against the knowledge of God. It's a fortified dwelling place where the enemy can operate in deception. A stronghold of the mind is a lie that the devil establishes in our thinking. It's a thought process we deem as true, but is actually false. We could say that strongholds are the lies of the enemy hiding in carnal human reasoning waiting for us to agree with them and approve of them by way of that humanistic mentality, and often causing us to be in agreement with the ways of the world. Once we've done that, we then unfortunately make choices filtered through those strongholds of lies. So, in the next chapters, let's discover, in more depth, what mindsets and strongholds are and how they are built so we can beware.

CHAPTER TWO

LIES AND MINDSETS

While seeking the Lord, He showed me that mindsets are a vast network, layers upon layers, connection upon connection, that are built up over time. They involve situations and circumstances encountered in a fallen world that get interwoven and reinforced by experiences that appear to be true, but obviously aren't "the Truth", the truth of God's Word, Jesus' truth, the truth of the Holy Scriptures. He showed me that the enemy subtly and craftily builds mindsets up in much the same way that Jesus builds His church and the members of it. Jesus teaches line upon line, precept upon precept, here a little there a little. It's like laying a firm foundation of truth first, then building more truth upon it once it's firmly established, then more truth upon that and so on. A little here and a little there. If a mason were to lay a foundation and immediately begin to build row of brick by row of brick upon it, without allowing the mortar to firm up, to dry and set, well, the whole thing would tumble over. There would be no strength to sustain the weight of the next row or layer. And even in our own individual walk with Jesus, we learn a little here and a little there, line upon line, precept upon precept, as He builds His church. And as He says, the gates of Hell will not prevail against it. The gates of Hell will not prevail against it for it will be strong, perfected, and not having spot nor wrinkle or any such thing. Meaning, it will be a mature church made up of mature people of God.

This corresponds in the natural realm with too much light is blinding. When we're in the dark and a spotlight is shined directly into our face, we can't see a thing, we're blinded by it. And in the spiritual realm, if the Holy Spirit were to reveal every single thing we're doing and have done wrong and everything we have to give up, give us all the chastisement we would ever receive and tell us every single thing we would need to learn all at once, every storm we would have to weather, every fire we would have to walk through, we would be deflated, overwhelmed, beat down, and therefore, ultimately reject His gift of salvation and call upon our lives. We would be blinded to the good news of the gospel. So, He rather shows us one area to be worked on, then once that is in alignment with Him and His Word, He'll then build upon that with positive reinforcements from His Word and with His presence in our lives as we grow and mature in Him. Then He'll reveal to us another area or thing, etc. Here a little, there a little. Just like the mason building a wall with brick and mortar, allowing the mortar to set before adding another row of bricks. It is the same in the natural with parents bringing up their children. They only give them information and tasks that fit the age they are in. Adult matters are too heavy for children to carry.

This also is the way the enemy works in building mindsets within us over time. Lie upon lie, deception upon deception, here a little, there a little. The Holy Spirit showed me that the enemy's building up of mindsets is much like a spider weaving its web. A spider first spins a single thread. The enemy will whisper a little lie to you that you unwittingly believe, then deceive you with another once you believe the first lie, as the spider spins another thread of the web, and another, and so on. Then, unfortunately, everything you see, hear, and experience is filtered through that lens, that prism, that mindset built up by the devil's lie, which in turn, reinforces the lie. A spider doesn't weave its web from just single threads. Once the laying out of the foundation – the single strands of the web – is complete, the spider then weaves reinforcement supports around a single thread, fortifying it and giving it strength. It then spins a thread from there to another strand and spins around it a reinforcement, and so on until the web is complete and strong enough to capture and hold its prey before it comes to suck the life-giving blood from it. When we hear or experience something that is filtered through the lie, it brings reinforcement to the lie as the enemy then whispers, "See, I told you!" Then, when you agree with that situation or experience, proving the lie to be true in your life, a strong reinforcement has been built and the mindset of that lie strengthens and that mindset becomes a stronghold.

As an example of this, the Lord has asked me to share how the lies of the enemy produced a mindset within me that became a stronghold within my life. It was slowly being built up in my life for over fifteen years and started when I was just a small child of five years of age. It was being built up lie upon lie, deception upon deception, here a little, there a little, like a scurvy spider weaving its web to snare me and keep me trapped within it in the hopes of completely devouring me later. It was the lie that I was unlovable, not worthy of love, and it wasn't anybody's fault but my own. No one was to blame except me, it's just who I was.

As I previously stated, it first started when I was five years old. It was fall, and I was about to start kindergarten. My mom had come home from shopping with brand new clothes both for my older sister and my younger brother. I was the only one of her three children who didn't get any new clothes. When I asked Mom why I didn't, she explained that money was tight and she wasn't able to buy clothing for all three of us. She shared with me that I could wear all of my sister's clothing that she had outgrown, but my sister didn't have anyone to pass down clothes to her, for she was the first born. She continued explaining that my brother got new clothes because he also didn't have anyone to pass on clothes to him, because he was a boy and both my sister and I were girls. This hurt my feelings because I was about to start school and my little brother wasn't and yet he got new clothes and I didn't. A voice in my head reasoned that I was about to start school and new clothes were important to make a good impression and if my mom really loved me, she would have made a way for me to have some new clothes too, just like she did when my sister started school, just like the moms of all my friends starting school. Now, being an adult with a household budget as well as being a mother too, I can understand the decision my mother made. It was very reasonable for the situation at the time. But as a little kid without adult reasoning capabilities, it simply meant I wasn't loved enough. First lie believed, first strand spun.

A few years later my parents divorced and my dad moved out of the house. Again, that voice reasoned that if my dad really loved me, he wouldn't have left. Another lie believed, another strand spun.

About a year and a half later, I went to spend the summer with my dad and his new wife in their new house on the lake. I was told if I didn't like it there, I could go back home with Mom and my brother and sister in Mom's new house. I liked it well enough because I loved living on the water, but really missed my mom, so I said I wanted to go back and live with Mom. I was told I couldn't and had to stay there. That voice said if Mom truly loved me, she would have taken me back and if my dad really loved me, he would have let me go. More lies told, more strands spun. About a year after that, I was told that I was going to be adopted by my dad and stepmom. I didn't want to be because Mom was my mom and no one could or would ever take her place in my heart. I was informed by all, that it was for my own good for legal reasons. That voice showed up again and told me another lie about not being loved and another strand was spun.

The following Christmas at my grandma's house, after all gifts were opened, my grandma and grandma's sister, my great aunt, called us outside. There in the front yard were two really awesome sleds. They were like a snowmobile and car. You sat inside them rather than on them and could steer them with a steering wheel or handle bars that turned the skis, like with a snowmobile. They were the coolest sleds I had ever seen in my life. But they weren't for me. One was for my sister and the other for my brother. When I asked why I didn't get one, I was informed that I got a lot of really nice and expensive things that my brother and sister didn't get because I lived with my dad who had much more money than Mom. I was heartbroken and there was that voice reiterating the lie that I wasn't loved. Another lie told and believed, and another reinforcement spun. Being an adult, I can look back at the situation and see how my grandma and aunt loved all three of us the same and therefore wanted us all to have things equally, so consequently, just wanted to shore things up. But back then, being just a kid, I didn't get it. To me, it was like I was overlooked, disregarded, not worth it, unloved, just like the voice told me. Then there was the time I was in the hospital having a tonsillectomy and my mom was there but left before I came to from the anesthesia. And the following lie believed that she didn't love me for if she did, she would have stayed so that I could have seen her. I needed her so much at that time.

Back at home, my adoptive mom became physically abusive to me. She hit, slapped, smacked, backhanded, and beat on me leaving a variety of physical evidence behind her. Obviously, she didn't love me, so the voice said. She made me drink liquid dish soap to the point of me vomiting bubbles, then after eating, vomiting up my food along with the bubbles. I was not able to hold anything down for over a twenty-four-hour span. The abuse continued even to the point of my being elected "most accident prone" in our mock elections in Jr. high school because of the stories I made up about how I got the injuries due to being so embarrassed and ashamed. I just couldn't let the other kids know that I was tainted, unlovable, damaged goods, nothing more than a throw away. Anyway, my dad didn't stop my adoptive mom from any of the abuse but rather just gave me money to buy whatever my heart desired after apologizing to me over what had happened each and every time. That voice popped up again telling me that if my dad really loved me, he wouldn't allow that abuse at the hands of my adoptive mom and if my real mom truly loved me, she would let me come back to live with her instead of suffering at the hands of my dad and adoptive mom. More lies, strands, reinforcements, and fortifications of the lie being spun.

Other reinforcements of the lie included hearing my adoptive mom tell her friend over the phone that she wished she had never taken me. Then there was the time I came through the front door after playing outside only to see, on the coffee table, a magazine my adoptive mom bought with a headline on the front cover reading, "The Wicked Stepchild." There also were times when I didn't get to go be with my mom on the weekend because she and my brother and sister were going on a camping trip or to an amusement park, etc. One time when I was pondering over all of these things, a voice in my head whispered to me that I was the common denominator in all of them. It wasn't my mom or dad or adoptive mom or grandma or aunt's fault at all. It was my fault. The truth of the matter was that I simply was unlovable. And I believed it.

There were other things that happened in my life growing up that strengthened that mindset as those experiences filtered through the past experiences stored up in my mind and even in my subconscious memory, through that strong web spun from lies and deception, here a little, there a little. So much so, that even on my wedding day at the church right before the ceremony, I freaked out and almost called it off. That voice in my head asked me why my husband-to-be really wanted to marry me, for it couldn't be because he loved me. I knew that I was unlovable. What did Bill really want from me? What would happen to me?

Thank the Lord I muscled through and escaped from the tangled web of lies, remembering that the Holy Spirit spoke a word to me and did tell me that Bill was the man I would marry when I first met him and so did go through with the ceremony, for he and I are in our 42nd year of marriage. And I praise God that in less than two years later, He sent Jesus to meet me in my bedroom one fateful night and began the process of delivering me and continued tearing down that web of lies, dismantling that mindset, that stronghold that had me in a spiritual death grip, with His truth, light, and love, as I shared in my first book, Forgiven and Not Forgotten.

Because the enemy subtly crafts his lies specifically for different individuals, my granddaughter has agreed to share with us what her mindset turned stronghold was like for her while suffering in the deep throes of depression. I cannot express how proud of her I am and continue to cover her in prayer, wrapping her up in the blanket of God's love, safety, protection, and peace. Her poignant description is as follows…

"I wish depression was not my ball and chain. At times it feels like my only friend while it convinces me to push away my real friends, it consumes me like a heavy black wave of uncertainty until I am certain depression is all I can feel. Some days it isn't strong enough to wash over me, no, it stays lurking in the shadows waiting for one tiny inconvenience to crack my defenses. It is not a feeling I can control, it has its own mind like it is its own sentient being. It's a monster with sharp betraying fangs and seemingly welcoming arms. I push for healing, it shoves back, wanting me to stay in the dark with it, it wants me to seek comfort, just let go and let it consume me but I refuse. I don't want to stay controlled by it but most days it seems like giving up would be better. It tries to seductively whisper sweet nothings of crushing phrases and words I know are not true, but depression knows how to twist lies into believable truths, it knows how to manipulate and warp my way of thinking. I cannot wait for the day it's smaller than I am so I can finally show it who is the real boss." ~ Rochelle Stokley

Not understanding about mindsets is one area where some of the church, the ecclesia, has done damage to itself and others. Several years ago, I heard of a program put on by a church to deliver youth from "the spirit of homosexuality." They claimed they could cast that demon out. Many parents who had teens confessing to be homosexuals brought their kids in to be delivered. Needless to say, it was a huge flop. It caused mental trauma to so many youths and gave the church a bad reputation of having no power of the Holy Spirit or God. The reason it failed so miserably is that homosexuality is not a demon, devil, or evil spirit that can be cast out, but a mindset turned stronghold by believing a lie. We are taught this in the Holy Scriptures. Romans 1:24-28 states, "Therefore God also gave them up to uncleanness, in the lusts of their hearts, to dishonor their bodies among themselves, who exchanged the truth of God for the lie, and worshipped and served the creature rather than the Creator, who is blessed forever. Amen. For this reason, God gave them up to vile passions. For even their woman exchanged the natural use for what is against nature. Likewise, also the men, leaving the natural use of the woman, burned in their lust for one another, men with men committing what is shameful, and receiving in themselves the penalty of their error which was due. And even as they did not like to retain God in their knowledge, God gave them over to a debased mind to do those things which are not fitting".

Notice the phrase, "who exchanged the truth of God for the lie." In other words, they believed the lie, they were deceived. Remember that mindsets are built up by lies and deception, here a little, there a little, and then choices are made through the filter of that lie, that mindset, that stronghold. Lies, mindsets, and strongholds cannot be cast out, but take dismantling by the opposing truths of God's Word. Sometimes that deliverance is quick and miraculous, but more times than not, it is dismantled by the truths of God in a process over time. The only one thing that these misguided ministers trying to cast out the "spirit of homosexuality" had right was the source of it, and that the source was from the devil. When Jesus was speaking to the Jews who did not believe Him, or stated another way, accused Him of lying, and sought to kill him, He told them in John 8:44 – "You are of your father the devil, and the desires of your father you want to do. He was a murderer from the beginning and does not stand in the truth, because there is no truth in him. When he speaks a lie, he speaks from his own resources, for he is a liar and the father of it." Here we learn that the devil is the father and source of all lies.

Next, let's take a look at a few things the Bible has to say about lies and deception. Colossians 2:8 says – Beware lest anyone cheat you through philosophy and empty deceit, according to the tradition of men, according to the basic principles of the world, and not according to Christ. Here, we learn that philosophy and the basic principles of the world are full of lies and deceit, and we should beware of this fact, lest a mindset be built up. 2 Thessalonians 2:9-12 reads, The coming of the lawless one is according to the working of Satan, with all power, signs and lying wonders, and with all unrighteous deception among those who perish, because they did not receive the love of the truth, that they might be saved. And for this reason, God will send them strong delusion, that they should believe the lie, that they all may be condemned who did not believe the truth but had pleasure in unrighteousness. This Scripture lets us know in no uncertain terms that if we continue on refusing the truth and believing the lies of the enemy, continuing on in deception, and persist in wrong mindsets thereby allowing them to become strongholds in our minds, marching on in unrighteousness, joining with others who believe the same lie, causing interconnected webs of lies with others, it won't end well for us. We've got to be careful on what we "set our minds" on and believe in our hearts. This is also why it is so vital for us to understand lies, mindsets, and strong-holds and recognize our need to be delivered from them.

In the next chapter, we'll delve into strongholds in more depth so that we can have a deeper awareness of them and be on guard against the lies and deception of the enemy, as well as learn why the enemy targets our minds.

CHAPTER THREE

UNDERSTANDING STRONGHOLDS

Before we get into strongholds in more depth, let's explore why the devil goes after our minds in the first place. It is because our mind is a part of us that was created in God's own image. Genesis 1:26 says – "Let Us make man in Our image, according to Our likeness…" Our minds are where God speaks to us Spirit to spirit, where we hear what His Spirit communicates to us, and where He reveals His will to us, otherwise known as that still small voice. The Word of God emphasizes our mind's importance in that it teaches us God renews our lives by renewing our minds and renews our minds through His truth. Romans 12:2 reads "And do not be conformed to this world, but be transformed by the renewing of your mind, that you may prove what is that good and acceptable and perfect will of God." Ephesians 4:23 instructs "and be renewed in the spirit of your mind." Jesus, while praying for His disciples in John 17:17, prayed "Sanctify them by Your truth, Your Word is truth."

See, if the devil can convince you to believe the lie, then he has established a foothold, has been given a place, like Ephesians 4:27 warns about. "Nor give place to the devil." And once he gets a place or a foothold, he will then try to work more in your life, feeding you more lies, bringing you more deception in the hopes of ultimately getting you to rebel against God. This is why the deceiver attacks our mind. And this is why we must meditate upon God's Word both day and night. It is so that when the lie comes to our minds, we will be able to recognize it and immediately cast that lie down, replace it with the countering truth of God's Word, and quickly slam that gate shut, the spiritual gateway to our thought processes!

We'll delve into this in more detail a little later, but before we do, let's look at another reason why the devil goes after our minds. Our minds are harbored in our brains and our brain is the command center of our person. Our brain gives the commands to our whole body in what it does. It commands to move, it commands to be still, it commands whether to move quickly or slowly and how to be still, whether to remain standing, to sit or to lie down. It comes up with what to say and in what manner, decibel, or tone in which to say it in. Or it instructs us to be quiet and not say a thing. It is what forms plans on how to accomplish something we've determined to do. These are just a few examples of how the brain is the control center of our bodies, our flesh. Generally speaking, the mind is the brain. The mind is the psychological term while the brain is the physiological term used to describe it.

We could also say that the brain or mind is the citadel of our soul, a fortress that commands, a stronghold. Our souls consist of not only our minds, but our will, and our emotions. Also, the mind is very instrumental in that it is the very battlefield that the devil and evil spirits yearn to capture. They know that if they can control the mind, they then can control the person. The enemy wants to capture the minds of the people because he who controls the mind, controls a very strategic place. Proverbs 16:32 shows us this. "He who is slow to anger is better than the mighty, And he who rules his spirit than he who takes a city." The word for spirit here in the original Hebrew references the mind. Also, Romans 8:5-6 says – For those who live according to the flesh set their minds on the things of the flesh, but those who live according to the Spirit, the things of the Spirit. Notice how the Scripture says, "set their minds". In other words, a mindset. We learned earlier that a mindset can become a stronghold, a habitual pattern of thought built up in one's thought life.

Next, let's look at Proverbs 23:7. It reads, "For as he thinks in his heart, so is he". Here we learn our perception, or what we think, is our reality and that the heart and mind are directly connected, that a person's thoughts are who they really are. Wow! Did you catch that? What we think of ourselves in our hearts, is who we really are, who we believe that we really are. So, if the father of lies deceives us into believing that we are a failure, then we become a failure in our heart and mind and don't succeed in anything we were attempting and even in some cases, subconsciously sabotage our own success. If the deceiver convinces you that you are ugly, then no matter what you do, whether it's a new haircut or color, whether you put on the latest trends in clothing, whether you get your teeth fixed, whether you exercise and tone or buff up your muscles, whether you diet and lose some weight, whether you have a mole removed or whatever you do in attempting to become attractive, in your heart and mind you are ugly, so to you, you are ugly. The enemy also works on the other end of the spectrum too. He can deceive you into believing that you are a perfect, wonderful, successful specimen of a person just as you are and have no need of God at all. That you can accomplish anything that you want to within your own power for after all, look what you've achieved already without Him. Look how free you feel. See how successful you are. Look at the people who are envious of what you have or who you are. The enemy's goal is to spiritually kill you, to steal salvation from you, and lead you to eternal destruction by leading you down the path of believing that all of that Bible stuff is just a bunch of hooey. And this is just how powerful our minds truly are.

Next, let's look at what Jesus said in Matthew 12:34-35, "Brood of vipers! How can you, being evil, speak good things? For out of the abundance of the heart the mouth speaks. A good man out of the good treasure of his heart brings forth good things, and an evil man out of the evil treasure brings forth evil things." Here a connection is made from the heart to the mouth, so we learn that the mind, the heart, and the mouth are all connected. And again, that is why the enemy wants to gain control of our thought life. Believe it or not, before we were saved, our minds were already held captive by the devil. It is actually what the Bible tells us. Look what Colossians 1:21 says – "And you, who once were alienated and enemies **in your mind** by wicked works…" (emphasis mine).

This just fascinates me for here we learn that we, before salvation, were enemies of God where? In our mind! And how? By way of our wicked works! Recall how our minds are the control center of our whole bodies and controls what we do with them. Also, in 2 Corinthians 4:3-4, Paul explains, "But even if our gospel is veiled, it is veiled to those who are perishing, whose minds the god of this age, (the devil) has blinded, who do not believe, lest the light of the gospel of the glory of Christ, who is the image of God, should shine on them." What I love is that when the light of Jesus shines within us, we believe and repent. In the original Greek, the word for repent is metanoeo and literally means to change one's mind and gain a new perception. And this reiterates how important our mind actually is.

And speaking of the light of Jesus shining into the darkness of this world and our unrepentant hearts and minds, we must understand that contrary to what literature has portrayed throughout the ages in all sorts of literary works, lightness and darkness are not two equal opposing forces. Opposing yes, but not equal. Light is always, and I repeat, always far more powerful than darkness. Darkness cannot continue in the presence of light. Think of when you come home late and the house is all dark so you then flip the switch to the overhead light on. What happens to the darkness? Or what happens to the dark night once the sun rises and dawn springs forth, shining her early light? And even in the very beginning, God separated the darkness from the light, the day from the night, by the rising of the sun. Light always has been and always will be more powerful than darkness. Darkness cannot continue to exist in light, but light continues to pierce through darkness every single time, completely eliminating it. This is an undisputable fact and the reason it is true is that Jesus Himself is the light.

We find that Isaiah prophesied it in the Old Testament 700 years before the birth of Jesus in Isaiah 9:2 – The people who walked in darkness have seen a great light; those who dwelt in the land of the shadow of death, upon them a light has shined. We find that Jesus himself declared it in John 8:12 – Then Jesus spoke to them again, saying, "I am the light of the world. He who follows Me shall not walk in darkness, but have the light of life." And when John was given a glimpse of heaven in the Spirit and saw the New Jerusalem descending out of heaven in Revelation 21:23, he conveyed to us, "The city had no need of the sun or the moon to shine in it, for the glory of God illuminated it. The Lamb is its light." Then John says in verse 25 that there shall be no night there, thus proving that light completely eliminates darkness. Thank you, Father God! Thank you, Jesus!

As mentioned briefly above, the way to change mindsets and tear down strongholds is by replacing the lies with the truth of God's Word. A stronghold is a fortified place. Remember the mindset turned stronghold in my mind as a young child was fortified by more lies being fed to me, that I believed, as I saw them through the lens of that original lie. And it was torn down, every lie, by the opposing truth of God's Word. We have to have our memory banks so full of the truth of the Word, that we are instantly able to cast foolish thoughts or lies down when the enemy whispers them to us, with the countering God truth of God's Word. I would like to add here that God's truth does include prophetic words spoken over us too, perhaps a word of knowledge or a word of wisdom, as well as us hearing God speak to us directly through His Holy Spirit, like when He spoke to me when I met my husband-to-be, that this man was the man whom I would marry.

The Holy Spirit showed me that meditating on the Scriptures is very much like a cow chewing its cud. A cow goes out in the field and grazes on the grass out in the field or meadow. That would be the equivalent of us reading the Bible. Then later, while relaxing, lying down in the shade perhaps, the cow regurgitates that grass and chews on it some more. That would be the equivalent of us thinking on and pondering over a particular Scripture or passages of Scripture. Or in other words, mentally chewing on them, contemplating on them, mulling them over, getting every last bit of truth out of them by revelation of the Holy Spirit just as a cow gets every last nutrient out of that grass, breaking it down further as it chews some more. When we do our mental chewing, the Word is being fortified not only in our minds, but in our hearts and within our spirits. So, we could say that the cow's masticating (a fancy word for chewing) is the same as our meditating.

I just have to veer off in another vein of the animal kingdom regurgitating for a moment, because it is so vitally significant. While the cow regurgitates to chew its cud, to continue to feed itself, other wild animals including fowl, regurgitate what they've eaten to feed their young. We must share and teach our young what we have learned from the Bible. In the case of my stronghold, the lies started at a very young age. The enemy sets out to trap our young in attempts to thwart the plans of God in our promised seed, the next generation. If I had been fed the truth of the Scriptures in a greater degree, then perhaps I could have countered and warded off the lies from becoming a stronghold in the first place. And I am quite confident that this is why God instructed Moses to teach the people in Deuteronomy 6:7. "You shall teach them diligently to your children, and shall talk of them when you sit in your house, when you walk by the way, when you lie down, and when you rise up." I also like the NLT version. It reads, "Repeat them again and again to your children. Talk about them when you are at home and when you are on the road, when you are going to bed, and when you are getting up." I really like the way they bring out to repeat them again and again to your children. It's like the cow bringing up its cud to chew on again and again. And as we do this, then God not only hides His word in our children's hearts, but ours as well like the psalmist says in Psalms119:11 – Your word I have hidden in my heart, that I might not sin against You. And in verses 15 and 16 – I will meditate on Your precepts, and contemplate Your ways. I will delight myself in your statutes; I will not forget Your word. If we meditate on and teach the Scriptures, not only will we not sin against God, but we will be able to cast down those high thoughts and lofty lies of the enemy the moment he whispers them to us because we have remembered God's Word.

Now, let's return to discovering the importance of our minds. I cannot emphasize enough how imperative it is to have our minds saturated with the Word of God, and be so thankful that we have God's Holy Spirit to help us in this arena. John 14:26 says, and this is Jesus speaking, "But the Helper, the Holy Spirit, whom my Father will send in My name, He will teach you all things, and bring to your remembrance all things that I have said to you." There are two things I'd like to bring out from this passage. First, the Holy Spirit will teach us. Where do we learn? That's right. In our brains or minds. The second thing is that the Holy Spirit will bring to our remembrance the things we learned. And where do we remember things? Again, in our minds.

Next, let's look at some more Scripture concerning our minds. Isaiah 26:3 says, "You will keep him in perfect peace whose mind is stayed on you." How do we keep our mind stayed on Him. We find that answer in Philippians 4:8 – Finally brethren, whatever things are noble, whatever things are just, whatever things are pure, whatever things are lovely, whatever things are of a good report, if there is anything praiseworthy – meditate on these things. And what does Jesus have to say about our minds? Matthew 22:37 – Jesus said to him, "You shall love the Lord your God with all of your heart, with all of your soul, and with all of your mind." Let us do as 1Peter 1:13 encourages us to do. "Therefore, gird up the loins of your mind, be sober, and rest your hope fully upon the grace that is to be brought to you at the revelation of Jesus Christ". Let's look at this verse in the Amplified Version, as it really brings it home for us. It reads, "So prepare your minds for action, be completely sober [steadfast, self-disciplined, spiritually and morally alert], fix your hope completely on the grace [of God] that is coming to you when Jesus Christ is revealed. I don't mean to be so redundant, but I cannot emphasize enough how our minds are so vitally important to our walk with God and our wellbeing, body, soul, and spirit.

In conclusion of this chapter, let's get back to strongholds. Another thing I love about the Holy Scriptures is that the word "stronghold" is used just once in a negative way, or as coming from the devil like when Paul says in 2 Corinthians 10:4-5, "For the weapons of our warfare are not carnal but mighty in God for the pulling down of strongholds, casting down arguments and every high thing that exalts itself against the knowledge of God, bringing every thought into captivity to the obedience of Christ". However, it is used many times in a positive way and references God as our stronghold. Psalm18:2 says – The Lord is my rock and my fortress and my deliverer; My God, my strength, in whom I trust; My shield and the horn of my salvation, my stronghold. We also have Nahum 1:7 that says, "The Lord is good, a stronghold in the day of trouble; and He knows those who trust Him." Other Scripture along the same lines use the word citadel, refuge, and fortress. The Bible also teaches many times over in the Old Testament that God destroyed the enemy's strongholds and fortified high places and those in turn became strongholds for the people of God. And that really is the whole point. Every negative mindset and stronghold that God delivers us from, then is transformed into a God stronghold for us. A high fortified place that cannot be taken by the enemy, a very strategic place, which is our minds once we have fortified them with the truth of the Holy Scriptures. Hallelujah! Praise the Lord!

CHAPTER FOUR

ERROR AND MISCONCEPTION

As this is a time where God is calling for maturity and is shining His light of truth into the error of deliverance, we would be remiss if we didn't look at some of the methodology, practices, and actions of the church in times past, and even in some cases, still ongoing in the present. Unfortunately, the church has spent centuries developing church philosophies, church theology, church discipleship, church practices, church programs, church membership rules, etc., but have completely neglected the area of deliverance, or on the flipside, have grossly mistaught about it. Therefore, many inexperienced and/or immature ministers have attempted deliverance and the casting out of demons, and in so doing, have done and said things contrary to the Word of God. The aftermath of this is that they not only produced ineffectiveness, but have imbued, in some cases, a sense of hopelessness in those they attempted to deliver, and even traumatized some of them. And worse yet, in attributing things to demons, when there was no involvement of them at all, they took away the recipient's personal responsibility, their self-control over their own lives, thereby preventing them from understanding that they needed to repent of and be delivered from some things, and allow God to do an ongoing, perfecting, maturing work in them.

Let's look at works of the flesh, for example. These misguided ministers in attempting to cast out works of the flesh after declaring a person to be demon possessed and under its control over them, took away the recipient's responsibility of self-control over their lives, minds, and emotions. They took away from the recipient, the responsibility of understanding and thereby acting upon Scripture that teaches we are to pick up our cross daily and thereby crucify our flesh daily. We'll cover the works of the flesh in a moment. Before we get into them, it must be stated that, as with all things, whatever the church teaches, preaches, and practices, must line up with the Scriptures of the Bible, including the arena of deliverance. Now let's look at Galatians 5:19-21. It teaches, "Now the works of the flesh are evident, which are adultery, fornication, uncleanness, lewdness, idolatry, sorcery, hatred, contentions, jealousies, outbursts of wrath, selfish ambitions, dissentions, heresies, envy, murders, drunkenness, revelries, and the like; of which I have told you beforehand, just as I also told you in time past, that those who practice such things will not inherit the kingdom of God." Next let's look at verses 24 and 25. "And those who are Christ's have crucified the flesh with its passions and desires. If we live in the Spirit, let us also walk in the Spirit."

I just want to touch on a few of the works of the flesh listed above so we can get an understanding that works of the flesh cannot be cast out. I've seen ministers trying to cast out the spirit of lust in the past, but lust is a flesh work and a heart condition that we ourselves must overcome. 1 John 2:15-16 reads – Do not love the world or the things in the world. If anyone loves the world, the love of the Father is not in him. For all that is in the world – lust of the flesh, the lust of the eyes, and the pride of life – is not of the Father but is of the world. And Jesus said in Matthew 5:28, "But I say to you whoever looks at a woman to lust for her has already committed adultery with her in his heart." In these two passages of Scripture, we see that lust is a flesh and a heart problem, not a "spirit' to be cast out. The same is true of the "spirit of anger" and "the spirit of jealousy" for instance, and of any other flesh work listed above because they are not unclean spirits, but works of the flesh. In Ephesians 4:26-27, Paul says to be angry and do not sin: do not let the sun go down on your wrath, nor give place to the devil. Notice he says don't give place to the devil. He doesn't mean to give the devil a place inside you to possess you, but to not give the devil a foothold in your thought life. In verse 29 he says let no corrupt word proceed out of your mouth. Remember, we learned the mind, mouth, and heart are all connected. In verse 31, he admonishes to let all bitterness, wrath, anger, clamor and evil speaking be put away from you with all malice. Malice basically means an evil mindset that works itself out in shrewd and deceitful calculation of doing another harm. Here we see that it is a mindset that needs to be corrected by the truth of God's Word, not of a need to be delivered from a demon. He then continues on in verse 32 saying to be kind to one another, tenderhearted, forgiving one another, even as God has forgiven us. Here we see that these are choices to be made and we make our choices within our minds.

I believe that immature ministers in trying to cast out demons that are not demons at all, and therefore cannot be cast out, most likely contributed to the errors in the deliverance arena where ministers went on for hours or days or even weeks, in some cases. That whole time of trying to deliver people from demons that weren't present, exasperated them. They believed the Scriptures where Jesus defeated the enemy and gave all authority over them to us, but in being "immature" in the things of the Spirit, but having a zeal for them, coupled with a lack of wisdom and discerning of spirits, made their efforts fruitless. It angered them as well, as they had their hearts and minds set on doing this for Jesus, the kingdom of God, and for the misguided recipient. Or in other words, a mindset. But the deliverance of the demon wasn't happening, so they got angry, yelled louder, screamed and shouted, turned all red in the face, had purple veins popping out from their neck and foreheads. They then began shaking in the midst of all this anger as they raised their fists in a show of authority and superiority over the demonic, causing beads of sweat to pop out on their foreheads and drench their whole bodies in it.

This, in turn, was causing them to huff and puff, and spit and sputter as they commanded and demanded the non-demons to come out while quoting Scripture over and over again. I'm sure they justified themselves in doing all of this by misunderstanding actual Scripture in the Bible. Perhaps Ephesians 6:12 that reads – For we do not wrestle against flesh and blood, but against principalities, against powers, against the rulers of the darkness of this age, against spiritual hosts of wickedness in the heavenly places. – Maybe they thought they had to literally wrestle against demons. Perchance from 1 Timothy 6:12 where it teaches to fight the good fight of faith, so they thought they had to literally fight with unclean spirits. Or maybe they thought of the Scripture where the disciples could not cast out a demon and Jesus said there are some that only come out with prayer and fasting in Matthew 17:12, so they decided to go pray and fast for the night and start up again the next day. Then somehow, this became the norm for the casting out of demons either by teaching or perhaps by others' observation of them performing these rituals causing the next generation to walk in error as well. Some ministers even developed programs and whole ministries around this and started advertising their services.

As a matter of fact, I remember seeing a newspaper advertisement regarding this some time ago. It advertised that demons afflicted and tormented and desired to destroy people by way of physical, spiritual, and emotional means. It went on to decree that demons wreak havoc in people by what the Bible calls "demonization". I thought that was odd since I couldn't seem to find that term in any of my different translation versions of the Bible at all. Anyway, it went on saying that when one is victimized by Satan, they are demonized. It then gave examples of one being demonized so you could know if this pertained to you, by giving a list of what I'll call symptoms or conditions. It listed things like hearing voices, having suicidal thoughts, intense fear or other intense negative emotions, deep depression, having nightmares, experiencing unexplainable pain, desiring to do bad things all of the time, among others. It then went on explaining that demons are able to enter us through cracks in our natural walls of resisting him. The Word does say to resist the devil and he will flee from you, but it does not say that if you don't resist the devil, he enters and demonizes you and then needs to be cast out of you. It then gave a list of things that made you high risk of being demonized that either you, your parents, or grandparents engaged in before! Included were occult things like astrology, palm readings, tarot cards, witchcraft, and Ouija boards. It also listed other things like either being a victim or perpetrator of sexual abuse, being involved in homosexuality, emotional trauma, and suffering mental illnesses such as dementia. And if that all wasn't bad enough, it decreed that Christians were not exempt! It then, of course, let you know that they could free you from all of this through the power of the Lord Jesus Christ. Just give them a call and they would set up a deliverance appointment with you.

The above is wrong on so many different levels. For one thing, as discussed in the first chapter, homosexuality is a mindset formed by believing a lie and cannot be cast out, but must be torn down by the truth of God's Word and a changing and resetting of the mind. Secondly, in the list of the works of the flesh from Galatians 5 listed above, we see that sorcery, which is used in witchcraft, is named as a work of the flesh, not a demon we need to be delivered from. And thirdly, I can guarantee you that deep depression is not a demon and I know this because there was a point in my life where I personally suffered from it. I no longer suffer from it and haven't for over forty years and absolutely no demon was cast out of me at all, not ever! I also wrote about this in my first book, Forgiven and Not Forgotten in detail, but I'll give you an abbreviated version of it so you can see what I mean.

After my parents were divorced when I was eight years old, I later moved in with my dad and his new wife about a year and a half later and subsequently was adopted by my stepmom, all against my wishes, mind you. I finally moved back in with my mom at seventeen, finished my senior year in high school, then traveled and settled down in Texas for a bit. When I encountered a bad situation there, I came back home to my mom's. Not long after that, she was killed in a car accident and I tumbled into a deep depression because I had only lived with her a few short years and was out of state for a large portion of that time. So, when she died, I was devastated. For three weeks I didn't do anything but cry, refusing to do things with my friends or anyone else, for that matter. I just wanted to be near my fiancé and was staying at his house. I didn't eat anything for those three weeks and lost a lot of weight.

Then one morning while coaxing me to eat, my then future mother-in-law spoke to me and it was if I heard both my mom and God speaking to me through her words. It was in that moment that I decided I was going to get out of the funk I was in and continue to live my life. I ate what was before me and then began planning my wedding. I went on with my life being the cheerful, happy, and upbeat person I was before the accident. That was all it took. If you'll notice, I said I heard God speak and then decided to stop living in that depression or in other words, I simply changed my mind and reset it in a different direction. The depression I was living in was a mindset, and I merely set my mind to do something else, meaning I repented of it, and by the grace of God, did it. Remember, the word repent in the original Greek means to change one's mind and since the mind and heart are connected, my heart changed along with my mind.

As I was contemplating over how easy it seemed to have misconceptions, misunderstandings, and out and out error passed on down through the church for years and generations even, the Holy Spirit brought back to my remembrance some incidents in my life to illustrate how easily this happens and as an example of trying to operate in the things of the Spirit, immaturely, as well. The examples I'm about to share with you really pale in comparison to the damage that has been done in the body of Christ through the years in this arena, and actually didn't cause any damage at all, thank the Lord, but are lighthearted illustrations that do demonstrate how it can occur.

While living with my dad and adoptive mom, I was brought up in an old-fashioned Pentecostal church, a church that not only believed in the demonic, but attributed just about any negative thing that occurred in one's life to the work of demons. They taught, and therefore my adoptive mom taught me, that there was a demon of "whatever" the bad thing was and we were being attacked by it whenever said bad thing occurred. But to fear not, because we had God-given power over the devil and demons in Jesus' name. They taught that all we had to do was say out loud firmly, "Satan, I rebuke you in the name of Jesus!" and that demon would have to flee from us and if it didn't at first, then we just had to repeat it again and again, continuing to command it until it recognized the God-given authority we had and obeyed, thus fleeing from us.

So, there I was, about eleven years old, setting out to do my chore. My chore was to burn all of the paper and cardboard trash in the burn barrel located in the backyard. It was the middle of winter and there was about eight inches of snow on the ground. Once I had dumped all of the trash into the burn barrel which was about half full of previously burned ashes, I ignited a newspaper on opposite corners with the lighter I was given to accomplish my chore. I had an old stick that I was to occasionally stir the fire with so that all of it would burn making sure the fire didn't go out before all of it was turned to ash. While I was stirring, a blustery wind came off the lake and picked up a section of newspaper still on fire. When the wind passed by and died down, the still burning clump of newspaper that was air born dropped to the ground behind me. When I turned around to see where it had landed, I saw that it had dropped at the back of my left boot and had ignited the back of my pants on fire!

I had on a pair of 100 percent polyester bellbottom pants. It was in the beginning of the 70s after all. When I saw my pants were burning, I remembered what I was taught and immediately started yelling, "Satan, I rebuke you in the name of Jesus." But I was still on fire, so I yelled it again, a little louder this time, "Satan, I rebuke you in the name of Jesus!" When I looked back again, I saw that the polyester bellbottom pant leg was melting right to my winter boot as it burned and had nearly reached the top of my boot. I knew that my leg would be next. At this point, I dropped to the ground, and began to roll over and over again through the snow. But I saw that my pants were still burning after rolling over numerous times when I checked to see if the fire had gone out. I next picked up handfuls of snow while lying on the ground and by throwing the snow over my burning, melting pants, was able to put the fire out, stopping its upward climb to my leg. After I put the fire out, I went inside and told and showed my dad what had happened and explained how I, myself, had to put out the fire with snow. He, after laughing, told me the devil had nothing to do with it, but it was just a naturally occurring chain of events. He then admonished me to be more careful next time.

Now, let's fast-forward years later to when I am a mother of three small children, two little girls and a small toddler boy, and attending the same type of church I was raised in. I was sleeping soundly in my bed but awoke to the sounds of my young daughters, ages five and seven, shouting about something. I got up out of bed, flicked the hallway light on, and continued down the hall toward their bedroom to see what was going on. I was hoping they weren't arguing over a toy or some other trivial thing in the middle of the night. When I got to their bedroom door, I could make out what they were yelling. I heard both of them in tandem shouting over and over again, "Satan, I rebuke you in the name of Jesus!"

I next opened their bedroom door and saw their dresser had been pulled away from the wall several inches and both of them standing on their beds shouting toward the dresser in between them. I asked them what was going on in a quiet and gentle manner in hopes of calming them down. My oldest explained to me that there were scratching noises coming from behind their dresser that woke them up. So, they, working together, pulled the dresser, bit by bit, away from the wall to see what it was. But once they pulled it away from the wall, they couldn't see anything behind the dresser although they still could very plainly hear the scratching. They then explained to me that because there was nothing to see, they knew it was the devil. I went over to the side of the dresser and listened intently and sure enough, there most certainly were faint scratching noises.

At this point, their dad had woken up and joined me in the room. He then clarified to the girls that there was a mouse in the wall and it was making the scratching noise, not a demon. He next knocked on the wall and the scratching stopped. He subsequently informed the girls that the noises stopped because he scared the mouse away and it scampered off showing them that the mouse was more afraid of them than they should be of it. He promised them he would get the mouse tomorrow and all would be well as he pushed their dresser back in place, then gently urged them to go back to sleep. I tucked them back into their beds, kissed their cheeks, told them I loved them, and then their dad and I quietly exited their room, closing the door behind us. When we ourselves got back into bed, we chuckled and shared with each other how cute it was that they recognized the power of Jesus' name and were acting upon it, then went back to sleep ourselves.

I want to point out here that I did not teach my girls to rebuke the devil in the name of Jesus. This means that they must have picked it up some other way. Perhaps from my adoptive mom, their grandmother, who taught me to say and do it. She babysat them quite often and we did spend a lot of time with her. Or perhaps during service from watching the altar up in front of the church throughout personal ministry time. There was quite a bit of that going on in the church. Or possibly, from some of the songs that were sung during praise and worship, or perchance, from one of their teachers during their Sunday School classes. I can't say for sure, but I can indeed say that they picked it up somehow and proceeded to act upon it.

Although the above incidents were lighthearted, if the teaching and believing that demons were responsible for every scary or negative experience that we encountered in life continued to be reinforced rather than corrected, fear could have taken root in our minds and spirits or worse. And again, they also illustrate how easily error can be picked up and carried on into next generations.

Now that we have covered some of the errors in the arena of deliverance, we'll next turn to the Word of God to see what the Scriptures teach about it in the lives of Jesus Himself and in the lives of His disciples. In the meantime, let's praise His Holy name for bringing us forth into maturity in this new time of His visitation on the earth and for continuing to build His church in unity, line upon line and precept upon precept! Thank you, Father!

CHAPTER FIVE

JESUS AND DEMON ENCOUNTERS

One of the times I was seeking the Lord in regard to writing this book, I heard the Holy Spirit speak, telling me to study the Scriptures of Jesus and demons and He would bring revelation concerning them as I did. Therefore, we must look to Jesus and His ministry here on earth as He encountered demons. As we do this, we are able to glean truths from them as the Holy Spirit gives us insight and revelation regarding them. In this manner, we'll be able to separate truth from error in that arena of ministry. We find Jesus encountering demons, casting out unclean spirits, as well as healing and curing people of them throughout the gospels. So, let's now take a look at some of them and see what we can learn from these encounters.

As we discussed in the last chapter, some ministers yell and shout at "demons" to come out of a person, even for days in some instances. But when we study the Scriptures about how Jesus Himself dealt with unclean spirits, we find something completely different, the opposite, actually. Let's look at Mark 1:23-26. It reads, Now there was a man in their synagogue with an unclean spirit. And he cried out, saying, "Let us alone! What have we to do with You, Jesus of Nazareth? Did you come to destroy us? I know who You are — the Holy One of God!" But Jesus rebuked him, saying, "Be quiet, and come out of him!" And when the unclean spirit had convulsed him and cried out with a loud voice, he came out of him. Next, let's continue on in Mark and go to chapter 9. Here we find a father ran up to Jesus explaining his son had a mute spirit. He went on expounding that whenever the evil spirit seized his son, it threw him down; he foams at the mouth, gnashes his teeth, and becomes rigid. The disciples brought the boy to Jesus and immediately the spirit convulsed him, and he fell to the ground and wallowed, foaming at the mouth. As they story continues to unfold, we find what Jesus did in verse 25 - …He rebuked the unclean spirit saying to it, "Deaf and dumb spirit, I command you to come out of him and enter no more!"

Then in verse 26, we find what happened next. – Then the spirit cried out, convulsed him greatly, and came out of him…

There are two points we need to take note of here. First, notice in both passages that Jesus "said" to the demons, not yelled, hollered, or shouted, but just merely spoke. Secondly, the demons involved in both instances are the ones who cried out in a loud voice. They were the ones throwing a fit and carrying on, not the One who was doing the casting out. Jesus just "said" as He commanded them. He said and the demons obeyed. Both of these were just one and done occurrences. As a matter of fact, you will find that every time Jesus spoke to cast demons out, He merely said and commanded them out. He didn't holler and get all worked up ready to do battle and fight or wrestle with them. But somehow, through the ages, the script was flipped, so to speak, causing that error to run rampant throughout the body of Christ. But let us praise His Holy Name as He shines His light of truth into the darkness of error, bringing us to maturity in Him!

Next, let's examine another incident where Jesus casts out demons. Through this particular occurrence, we garner many things as we find it recorded by three of the disciples who all give an account from their own personal perspective and therefore bring out different little nuggets or tidbits within them. Let's start with the account in Mark 5:1-7. It reads, Then they came to the other side of the sea, to the country of the Gadarenes. And when He had come out of the boat, immediately there met Him out of the tombs a man with an unclean spirit, who had his dwelling among the tombs; and no one could bind him, not even with chains, because he had often been bound with shackles and chains. And the chains had been pulled apart by him, and the shackles broken in pieces; neither could anyone tame him. And always, night and day, he was in the mountains and in the tombs, crying out and cutting himself with stones. When he saw Jesus from afar, he ran and worshipped Him. And he cried out with a loud voice (there is a demon crying out in a loud voice again) and said, "What have I to do with You, Jesus, Son of the Most High God? I implore you by God that You do not torment me."

Here we find that the demon recognized Jesus immediately, called Him by name, and worshipped Him. I am reminded of the Scripture passage in Philippians 2:9-11 that proclaims every knee will bow, in heaven, on, and under earth, and that every tongue confess that Jesus Christ is Lord to the glory of God. It's exactly what this demon did. Also, it begs Jesus not to torment it. Here, I'm reminded of when Jesus triumphed over all powers and principalities by disarming them and then making a public spectacle of them from Colossians 2:15.

Continuing on in verses 8-13 – For He "said" to him, "Come out of the man, unclean spirit!" Then He asked him, "What is your name?" And he answered saying, "My name is Legion; for we are many." Also, he begged Him earnestly not to send them out of the country. Now a large herd of swine was feeding there near the mountains. So, all the demons begged Him, saying, "Send us to the swine, that we may enter them." And at once Jesus gave them permission. Then the unclean spirits went out and entered the swine (there were about two thousand); and the herd ran violently down the steep place into the sea, and drowned in the sea.

There are a couple of things we are able to glean from this. Here, we find Jesus asked for the demon's name. It's the only time Jesus asked a name of an unclean spirit and there was a distinct purpose for it. Jesus knew there were many evil spirits in the man and that there were many swine. Jesus also knew what was going to happen with a particular outcome in mind which we'll cover in a bit. It was not to set precedence for upcoming disciples and ministers to ask names of demons and conversate with them. In all other incidents, Jesus commanded and demons came out, showing the authority Jesus had over them and would later give to His disciples and all future followers.

The next thing to note is that Jesus gave them permission. This shows that the devil and his unholy angels must have permission to act. We also find this in Job where Satan asked and God gave permission to him to afflict Job, but also set boundaries that Satan had to abide by, telling him what he couldn't do. Through this, Job learned more about the awesomeness of God, got to know

God better personally, and God then blessed him with a double portion of what he originally had lost. Also, we find that Satan asked permission to sift Peter as wheat. We know permission was given because Jesus told Peter that when he returned, he was to strengthen his brethren. God allowed Peter to be sifted in order to mature him and show him that he couldn't do what Jesus was calling him to do in his own strength, might, and forceful disposition as he supposed he could. But rather, he would accomplish his calling by the strength and might of the Spirit of the Lord, the Holy Spirit that would be given to him later at Pentecost. And what we also learn from this is that all of the demonic are under God's and the Son of God's complete control and are merely vessels He uses to teach and strengthen those that He has called for His good purposes, and theirs as well. There is always a God ordained good purpose for demonic activity. They're just a tool in His toolbox, so to speak, as He works in our lives and teaches and matures us. Therefore, unclean spirits are nothing to fear at all. God and Jesus reign over them all and they must obey!

Next, we'll go to the Matthew account and glean a little more insight from his recording of this occurrence. In chapter 8, verse 29, we find that they cried out saying, "What have we to do with You, Jesus, You Son of God? Have You come here to torment us before the time?" What we learn from this, is again, to everything there is a season, a time for every purpose under heaven. They obviously knew there was a set time for their torment and that it wasn't that time yet.

In the Luke account, we learn even a little more. In chapter 8:28 we read, When he saw Je-sus, he cried out, fell down before Him, and with a loud voice said, "What have I to do with You, Jesus, Son of the Most High God? I beg You, do not torment me!" Then in verse 30 we find – Jesus asked him, saying, "What is your name?" And he said, "Legion," because many demons had entered him. – Now look at this, as we get a little more information. Verse 31 states, And they begged Him that He would not command them to go into the abyss.

Here we learn that the demons knew what their torment was to be. The abyss. In Matthew chapter 25, we see Jesus teaching that as He judges the nations, He will separate the people from one another as a shepherd separates the sheep from the goats, with the sheep at His right hand and the goats at the left. In Verse 41, Jesus says, "Then He will also say to those on the left hand, 'Depart from Me you cursed, into the everlasting fire prepared for the devil and his angels:'" Then Revelation 20:10 reads, The devil, who deceived them, was cast into the lake of fire and brimstone where the beast and the false prophet are. And they will be tormented day and night forever and ever. There is a set time for their everlasting torment, but it isn't until God has utilized them for all of His good works and plans until Jesus returns for His saints.

Now let's return to Mark for the rest of the account. We pick up in Chapter 5, verses 14 -20. So those who fed the swine fled, and they told it in the city and in the country. And they went out to see what it was that had happened. Then they came to Jesus, and saw the one who had been demon possessed and had the legion, sitting and clothed and in his right mind. And they were afraid. And those who saw it told them how it happened to him who had been demon possessed, and about the swine. Then they began to plead with Him to depart from their region. And when He got into the boat, he who had been demon possessed begged Him that he might be with Him. However, Jesus did not permit him, but said to him, "Go home to your friends, and tell them what great things the Lord has done for you, and how He has compassion on you." And he departed and began to proclaim in Decapolis all that Jesus had done for him; and all marveled.

See, Jesus wasn't in the city where many people were. He was in the countryside with fewer people there. In knowing that about 2,000 swine running into the sea and drowning was a huge event, He knew that it would spread, and spread quickly. Those who saw and lost their swine became afraid and spread what had happened from their perspective, one of fear and loss. So, the people from the city and country came to see what they had heard, and found Jesus and the once severely possessed man now in his right mind. And out of that fear, they began to plead that Jesus leave. But Jesus had a plan to overcome that. When the now healed man wanted to come with Je-sus, He didn't allow him to come, but asked him to go home and tell everybody what great things God had done. And all marveled. Through the miraculous state of the priorly terribly demon possessed man, the good news of God's love and compassion was spread throughout the country. The whole country who wasn't present for the event, now learned of Jesus and perhaps had seeds planted within their hearts for later occurring events. But not of the fear and loss others were spreading. Thank you, Lord! In getting back to the demons, Jesus was not going to send them to the abyss for eternal torment yet because they are under God's control for His use as He utilizes them for His good purposes and for the good of so many others.

As a matter of fact, every time Jesus cast out or healed someone from demons, it had a distinct God good purpose other than bringing deliverance for the afflicted. In Matthew 12:22-23 we find a good God purpose. It teaches, Then one was brought to Him who was demon possessed, blind and mute; and He healed him, so that the blind and mute man both spoke and saw. And all the multitudes were amazed and said, "Could this be the Son of David?" So here, multitudes of people's hearts and minds were being opened to the possibility that the promised Messiah had arrived and was among them. Back in the first chapter of Mark, after Jesus cast out an unclean spirit in verses 27-28, we find that afterward, the people were all amazed, so that they questioned among themselves, saying, "What is this? What new doctrine is this? For with all authority, He commands even the unclean spirits, and they obey Him." And immediately His fame spread throughout all the region around Galilee. In verse 34 we find that Jesus didn't allow the demons that He was casting out to speak, because they knew who He was. Then in verses 38-39 we find Jesus telling of a God good purpose, saying to some of His disciples … "Let us go into the next towns, that I may preach there also, because for this purpose I have come forth." And He was preaching in their synagogues throughout all Galilee, and casting out demons. Also, it says in Matthew 8:16 – When evening had come, they brought Him many who were demon possessed. And He cast out the spirits with a word, (Did you catch that? With just a word.) and healed all who were sick. Then in verse 17, we find a

God ordained good purpose. – that it might be fulfilled which was spoken by Isaiah the prophet, saying: "He Himself took our infirmities and bore our sicknesses."

I'd like to add one more account before we move on. When the Pharisees were accusing Jesus of casting out demons by the ruler of the demons, Beelzebub, He told them that couldn't be true, for a house divided against itself cannot stand. He then continued in Luke 11:20, "But if I cast out demons with the finger of God, surely the kingdom of God has come upon you." Here we find another good God purpose for Jesus casting out demons, to make known that the Kingdom of God is near and by which Spirit Jesus does cast demons out. By the finger of God. The Pharisees and Sadducees and all of the students of the law would have known quite clearly that Jesus was saying He operated in the supernatural power of God because the finger of God reference was spoken about twice before in the Old Testament Book of Exodus in regards to Moses' ministry. The first regarding when the Pharoah's magicians referred to the plagues God sent on Egypt as by the finger of God, and the second regarding the ten commandments being written with God's finger. Therefore, they most certainly would have known that Jesus was speaking of God's supernatural power, for they prided themselves on intimately knowing and teaching the Old Testament and the laws therein. They, however, could not operate in God's supernatural power, and feared that the great system of their manmade traditions that lacked God's supernatural power, would be torn from them.

After the Lord had shown me all of this, the incident involving the Phoenician woman's daughter and the children's bread, kept coming back into my mind for several days. I asked Him why He kept reminding me of it and He asked me to go back and read the Scripture passages. It was then, while reading them, that the Holy Spirit shined light onto the fact that Jesus did not speak one word, and yet assured the woman that her daughter was healed because the demon had gone out from her. I pondered for several more days over the demon being gone but not a word was spoken by Jesus. I kept re-reading those passages hoping to glean more from them when I heard the Holy Spirit speak. He asked me to recall the times I, myself, encountered and saw demons as He allowed me to see into the spiritual realm, and so I did. He then asked me a question. He asked me if I ever spoke a word to them. I answered Him that I did not. He responded with, "And yet they all fled, didn't they?" Wow! In that moment, I understood that the Holy Spirit was letting me know that the demons fled in fear without me saying a word and it was because they recognized Jesus in me and most certainly knew the authority Jesus had over them, and so they beat it out of there, not wanting to be tormented before their time, just like those demons Jesus encountered in His time!

I'll share the very first instance of seeing a demon with you as the Lord has asked of me, so you can understand what He was revealing. The first time the Lord opened my eyes to see into the spiritual realm to see a demon, was right after I had rededicated my life to Him in my early twenties. I had just recently been baptized in the Holy Spirit after my water baptism and was at home doing laundry. While my baby was napping, I went downstairs to the basement where the washer and dryer were with a load of assorted baby clothes, spit up bibs, booties, and blankets in my arms. When I stepped off the last step and turned to my left to make my way to the washing machine, there in the old olive-green wooden rocking chair my grandmother had given me, was a demon rocking. The moment I saw it, several things simultaneously occurred. I became nauseated, the hairs on my body rose, and the beating of my heart went into overdrive, racing, revving, urging me to take off. What I saw, was a big stocky, scraggly creature. The nearest thing I could liken it to was an abnormally large cat. Its fur was rather unusual as it had patches of different colored fur all in different lengths, some short, some long, the colors including, black, gray, yellow, orange and several different shades of brown. There wasn't a pattern at all, it just looked like it got dirty left-over scraps to put it all together. Some of the patches were matted, some tufted, and some sleek. It had large paws and long black claws that reminded me of a bear's paw and claws.

At that moment, it turned its head toward me and we made eye contact, its creepy yellow eyes glowing. It then immediately leapt up and jumped off the rocking chair, fleeing. It totally disappeared from my sight right before it hit the basement floor. It was just gone, having disappeared. Although I couldn't see it any longer, I could see that the rocking chair was still rocking from the inertia created when it jumped down, and I watched as that old fashioned rocker then gradually slowed and then stopped all motion. Seeing that demon was just several scant seconds, mind you. I didn't even have time to think of what I was going to do before it fled. So, I just continued making my way to the washing machine, praying in the Spirit, and loaded it up as usual. I'm pretty sure when I went back up the stairs, I moved just a little bit faster than before though, if I'm being honest.

I really didn't know what to make of it, so I just carried on and thought of it from time to time, wondering about it, but never seeking the Lord as to why He allowed me to see it or the others throughout my life, never knowing that He would utilize that first experience for such a time as this, as He was leading me to write this book. The Lord asked me to share this very first instance with you because I was relatively new in learning and understanding the Scriptures, other than the basics, and didn't even realize what it meant that Jesus had given all authority to us over the enemy as He proclaimed in Luke 10:19. He said, "Behold, I give you the authority to trample on serpents and scorpions, and over all the power of the enemy, and nothing shall by any means hurt you." This first experience of me seeing a demon, illustrates the fact that all unclean spirits know Jesus and the authority He has over them and recognizes Jesus has given it to us, even when we don't, just yet. Hallelujah!

After I pondered on all of the times God had opened my eyes to see in the spiritual realm, allowing me to see unclean spirits, I subsequently began remembering how many times I found, in the Scriptures, that when demons came into the presence of Jesus, they automatically fell down before Him, worshipped Him, and professed He was the Son of God, before the time He began to forbid them to speak. Anyway, those instantaneous acts of reverence toward Jesus proves His complete authority over all of them and their predetermined eternal submission to Him. They knew who Jesus was and because of that knowledge, they had no choice but to submit to His authority. We must never forget that it is in the name of Jesus, His name, being the source by which all power and authority lie. Thank you, Father! Thank you, Jesus!

In the next chapter, we'll look at the ministry of the disciples and see what we can ascertain from them as the Holy Spirit gives us understanding.

CHAPTER SIX

DISCIPLES, DEMONS, AND BEYOND

After Jesus chose and called his disciples and they walked with Him for a while, listening to His every word, seeing all of His miraculous works and learning much from Him, Jesus sent them out two by two. We find this in Mark. Mark 6:7 reads, And He called the twelve to Himself, and began to send them out, two by two, and gave them power over unclean spirits. Then we find in verses 12-13 what happened on their maiden launch. So, they went out and preached that people should repent. And they cast out many demons, and anointed with oil many who were sick, and healed them. Luke 9:1 also gives this account. – Then He called His twelve disciples together and gave them power and authority over all demons and to cure diseases.

Shortly thereafter, in Luke 10:1 we find Jesus sent out others, two by two, also. It reads, After these things the Lord appointed seventy others also, and sent them out two by two before His face into every city and place where He Himself was about to go. Then in verses 17-20, we find out what happened as they returned to Jesus. – Then the seventy returned with joy, saying, "Lord, even the demons are subject to us in Your name." And He said to them, "I saw Satan fall like lightening from heaven. Behold, I give you the authority to trample on serpents and scorpions, and over all of the power of the enemy, and nothing shall by any means hurt you. Nevertheless, do not rejoice in this, that the spirits are subject to you, but rather rejoice because your names are written in heaven." – Now let's look at the details of this passage. First, I'd like to draw your attention to the first verse of chapter 10 where it says that Jesus sent them out to every city that He Himself was about to go. In sending them out before He arrived Himself, He had them breaking up the fallow ground in people's minds and hearts, causing those they ministered to, to become fertile soil in which He could plant the seeds of the kingdom of God later, when He arrived there. The disciples spoke of Jesus with signs and wonders accompanying them and Jesus came afterwards speaking of God – His Father in heaven, Himself, and the kingdom of God.

Next, notice what Jesus said about the demons being subject to them in His name. He told the seventy that He saw Satan fall from heaven like lightening. As I pondered on this, the Holy Spirit gave me a vision of a lightning bolt coming from thick gray and black clouds in the midst of darkened skies and heading toward the earth in the middle of a thunderstorm. He then asked me if it scared me to see lightening in a thunderstorm. I answered that it didn't because it happens all of the time whenever there was a predicted thunderstorm. I told Him that I actually expected to see lightening as a part of it since it was just part of a naturally occurring chain of events. And in that moment of answering Him, I understood what He was teaching. He was pointing out that the enemy isn't in heaven, for he fell from there, but on the earth, in the world. The devil is actually referred to as the god of this world in 2 Corinthians 4:4. So therefore, it is just a naturally occurring thing that all of the enemy is subject to the authority of Jesus, Lord of heaven and earth, King of all kings, and Lord of all lords. He was training those disciples that they should expect to see that submission to His name as a naturally occurring thing, for He had given them power over all the enemy and nothing from the enemy could or would ever hurt them because of it. Wow!

Next, Jesus said that they shouldn't rejoice in the spirits being subject to them, but rejoice that their names were written in heaven. Here, Jesus is drawing their attention away from earthly things and the enemy to heavenly things and God the Father, for that is what was of importance here. He wants to shift their focus back to the kingdom of God in heaven. He wants them to be heavenly minded, to focus on the ministry or mission from heaven, here on earth, that they were created for and called to. Focus on God, not on demons. This lets us know in no uncertain terms that there should never be a "ministry of casting out demons", but ministry of proclaiming the good news of the coming of Jesus, and that the kingdom of God is at hand. Jesus was teaching that they should be focused on Father God's business and know that He has made a way for their deliverance from the world and worldly things, including demons.

And, as if all of that wasn't awesome enough, the Holy Spirit also expounded upon and gave me understanding about the act of falling. During hand-to-hand combat, the loser "falls" in battle like when David slew Goliath. Then later, when the Israelites fought against the Philistines and Jonathan was slain and King Saul fell upon his own sword, David lamented, "How the mighty have fallen in the midst of battle!" in 2 Samuel 1:25. So when we put all of this together, we learn that every time we go through a storm of life with our minds stayed on heavenly things, on the goodness of God and Jesus, and continue to be about our Father's business alongside of Jesus, resisting the storms of the devil, we defeat our enemy and he falls. It's just a naturally occurring thing that we come through the storms of life as overcomers and victors! Every time we overcome the storms, plots, plans, schemes, and traps the enemy has devised against us, he falls, his plans against us fail and we prevail! We should expect the enemy to fall whenever and wherever we go about kingdom business with our minds focused on the things of God. Jesus has proclaimed that He is building His church and the gates of Hell will not prevail against it! He also says that no weapon, no, not one weapon, will prosper against us. Jesus encourages us when He shares with us that He witnessed Satan fall! The devil is a defeated and fallen foe! Hallelujah! Also, right after speaking to the returned seventy in Luke 10:21 Jesus rejoices. It reads, In that hour Jesus rejoiced in the Spirit and said, "I thank you Father, Lord of heaven and earth, that you have hidden these things from the wise and prudent and revealed them to babes. Even so, Father, for so it seemed good in Your sight."

Now, let's review the Matthew 17:14-23 account of Jesus casting out the demon from an epileptic boy after his father brings the boy to Jesus. At this point, we already know that the disciples had gone out and were ministering to others in the name of Jesus and casting out unclean spirits successfully. However, they have now encountered one that they couldn't cast out. When the father brought the boy to Jesus, he told Him that he had at first brought the boy to the disciples, but they couldn't cast it out. Jesus sounds a little exasperated with the disciples when He answered and said, "O faithless and perverse generation, how long shall I be with you? How long shall I bear with you? Bring him here to Me." I believe this exasperation was because Jesus was expecting some growth, some maturity within His disciples, which we'll see in just a moment. Then Jesus rebuked the demon and the boy was cured right then and there. Later, when the disciples were alone with Jesus, they asked Him why they couldn't cast that demon out. Jesus explained to them it was because of their unbelief, their lack of faith.

What? Wait! Hadn't they already been casting out unclean spirits and healing the sick? Didn't that take faith? Yes! So, what is going on here? Well, the answer is that the disciples were no different than you or I. How many times in our own lives have we experienced God get us through difficult and seemingly impossible situations after we first believed, but later on, an even greater situation arose in our lives, one that appeared unsurmountable to us and we somehow didn't have big enough faith for this one? So, we cried out to God wavering in our faith, hoping, and yet disbelieving, and crying out in prayer to God, yet again. Time passes and the situation is still ongoing and appearing even worse. So, we desperately pray some more as doubt slowly creeps in because it appears that disaster is imminent, just looming on the horizon. But then God comes through right at the midnight hour. As a result, our faith was stretched, our faith was exercised, and our faith grew and strengthened, and we, therefore, grew up some in the Lord, we matured from it. And it happened again, and again, and so on, throughout our lives, until we were no longer babes in Christ. It is all about God working a maturing process within us, preparing us for the good plans He has for us in our future walk with Him. And that is exactly what Jesus was doing here.

In verse 21, Jesus, after He admonished them for not having the faith enough to cast this one out says, "However, this kind does not go out except by prayer and fasting." We really don't know about the demons the disciples encountered while out two by two on their own, because the Bible doesn't go into details about those encounters much, other than stating they cast out unclean spirits. So perchance, this demon appeared stronger than the others to the disciples, more ferocious. This one was throwing the boy into fire and water appearing as though it was trying to literally kill the boy, literally burn him up or drown him. Mark 9:22 shows us this as the father of the boy is speaking to Jesus – "And often he has thrown him both into the fire and into the water to destroy him. But if You can do anything, have compassion on us and help us." So, as this one looked greater and more powerful, it, in turn, most likely intimidated them, causing their faith to dwindle and their minds to doubt.

As I read what Jesus answered them with, the phrase "this kind" seemed to just jump off the page and so I was fixated on it. This kind. This kind? What kind? And as I contemplated over it, the answer came. An object lesson kind, a faith stretching kind, a maturing moment kind, a tool in God's toolbox kind. Jesus was about to teach them how to grow in maturity and gain greater faith by walking closer to and with God, thereby becoming more intimate with Him. Jesus continued explaining that this kind doesn't go out except by prayer and fasting. So, let's examine prayer and fasting. When we pray, we are seeking God and expecting to come into His presence. We spend one-on-one time with Him, and we speak with or cry out to Him. We praise His name. We worship Him and lift His name on high. We bow down before Him. Then we await His answer. We expect Him to respond because He says to draw near to Him and He will draw near to us. So, prayer time is about an intimate and private conversation with Him in our secret place. And when we are finished, after hearing from Him and experiencing His presence, we are strengthened, encouraged, peaceful, expectant, and full of hope. Fasting is when we give up things in our natural life to strengthen and build up our spiritual life. We fast from those things and redirect and dedicate our time spent on those activities to spending even more time with Him whether it's in prayer or studying His Word, or listening to sermons, for example. We crucify our flesh in so doing, and we allow our spirit man to grow stronger than our flesh man. We shift our focus from ourselves to Him and His kingdom and we grow up in maturity a little bit more.

We must understand that this is always an ongoing process throughout our lives. It is Jesus building His church with us being members of it in particular. We should never think that we have achieved all God has for us because His Word says, eye has not seen, nor heard, nor have entered into the heart of man the things God has prepared for those who love Him. This is true of every step all throughout our walk with Him. God always has more for us, but we have to be matured to the point to receive what He has for us in each season of our life. This is what Jesus did with His disciples and continues to do with us.

Let's now fast-forward and look into the future and see how this worked in the lives of the disciples, the end result, so to speak. We know they listened intently and took heed to what Jesus was teaching them and they matured in Him, indeed. They allowed the Lord to do that perfecting and maturing work within them. As an example, we can turn to Acts 5:12-16 and get a glimpse of it – And through the hands of the apostles many signs and wonders were done among the people. And they were all with one accord in Solomon's Porch. Yet none of the rest dared join them, but the people esteemed them highly. And believers were increasingly added to the Lord, multitudes of both men and women, so that they brought the sick out into the streets and laid them on beds and couches, that at least the shadow of Peter passing by might fall on some of them. Also, a multitude gathered from the surrounding cities to Jerusalem, bringing sick people and those who were tormented by unclean spirits, and they "all" were healed. I just want to point out a couple of things here. First, Peter went from laying on hands and anointing with oil for healing and curing and deliverance from unclean spirits in his maiden launch, to just having his shadow pass over people resulting in them being healed and cured. That is most definitely a matured result and reminiscent of people just wanting to touch the hem of Jesus' garment, and after doing so, were healed.

We can also take a peek at the maturing result of the apostle Paul. He didn't walk with Jesus as the disciples did. He didn't hear all of the parables and lessons that Jesus taught the other disciples – matured into apostles. He didn't see first-hand all of the miracles that

Jesus wrought. He didn't know Jesus, God in the flesh, person to person, and face to face as the disciples did, but went through a different process which we'll cover in the next chapter. But after that process of Paul growing and maturing in the Lord, we find similar results. He first started preaching and giving his testimony of what Jesus had done for him in the synagogues. The Bible tells us he then increased all the more in strength, and confounded the Jews, who formerly didn't believe Jesus was the Messiah, the Son of God in the flesh, who dwelt in Damascus, proving that Jesus is the Christ. Plots were made to kill him just as plots were made to kill Jesus and His disciples also, but by the grace of God and the working of the Holy Spirit, he escaped with the help of the disciples. After Paul was finally accepted by the other disciples and received His commission from God, he went about preaching Jesus and ministering to others amidst many trials, tribulations, strife, stoning, and suffering. Then, just as with Peter, we find something similar occurring after Paul's walk of maturation in the Lord in Acts 19:11-12. Now God worked unusual miracles by the hands of Paul, so that even handkerchiefs or aprons were brought from his body to the sick, and the diseases left them and the evil spirits went out of them.

If you'll notice, after a maturing walk of the disciples, especially of Peter, and also with Paul, they were brought to the place of miracles, signs, and wonders following them in most unusual ways. But it was only after a God ordained process. As discussed earlier in this chapter, we are no different than the disciples were, nor they from us, therefore, we should understand that God has a process for each and every one of us to bring us to that place of miracles, signs, and wonders following us as we go about the Father's business and are heaven and kingdom minded. And as we are members in particular of Jesus' church, understand that as we allow God to teach and train and mature us, then the whole called and chosen church, the remnant of the ecclesia, is brought into that maturity in the unity of His Spirt. I speak of the remnant because unfortunately, there will always be "Pharisees and Sadducees" among us in the church, just as Jesus taught in the parable of the wheat and the tares. Let's take a look at it.

Mathew 13:24-30 reads – Another parable He put forth to them saying: "The kingdom of heaven is like a man who sowed good seed in his field; "but while men slept, his enemy came and sowed tares among the wheat and went his way. But when the grain had sprouted and produced a crop, then the tares also appeared. So, the servants of the owner came and said to him, 'Sir, did you not sow good seed in your field? How then does it have tares?' He said to them, 'An enemy has done this.' The servants said to him, 'Do you want us then to go and gather them up?' But he said, 'No, lest while you gather up the tares you also uproot the wheat with them. Let both grow together until the harvest, and at the time of harvest I will say to the reapers, "First gather together the tares and bind them in the bundles to burn them, but gather the wheat into my barn.""""

Now let's look at the explanation Jesus gives to His disciples in verses 36-43 – Then Jesus sent the multitude away and went into the house. And His disciples came to Him, saying, "Explain to us the parable of the tares in the field." He answered and said to them: "He who sows the good seed is the Son of Man. The field is the world, the good seeds are the sons of the kingdom, but the tares are the "sons of the wicked one". The enemy who sowed them is the devil, the harvest is the end of this age, and the reapers are the angels. Therefore, as the tares are gathered and burned in the fire, so it will be at the end of this age. The Son of Man will send out His angels, and they will gather out of His kingdom all things that offend, and those who practice lawlessness, and will cast them into the furnace of fire. There will be wailing and gnashing of teeth. Then the righteous will shine forth as the sun in the kingdom of their Father. He who has ears to hear, let him hear!"

We know the Pharisees and Sadducees are children of the devil as we learned back in chapter two in John 8:44 when Jesus said to the Jews – "You are of your father the devil, and the desires of your father you want to do. He was a murderer from the beginning and does not stand in the truth, because there is no truth in him. When he speaks a lie, he speaks from his own resources, for he is a liar and the father of it." We also know that the devil and unclean spirits can only do as God allows as He rules them and He utilizes them as tools to bring about His good God purposes. The enemy will be here until the end of this age when Jesus returns for His church, the remnant, and the unclean spirits know they have a set time for this. They'll be here until God's good purposes with them are complete. God isn't going to throw away His tools until He has finished building His kingdom, for if He did, then some of His "wheat" couldn't be harvested, for they, as the young, tender, babe stalks of wheat would have been uprooted and lost. And Jesus isn't going to get rid of His tools until His church is built to perfection. That would be the equivalent of the mason, discussed in chapter two, throwing away his mortar, bricks, and trowel before his wall was completely built. God the Father and God the Son have Their process and take us through ours. So, let's continue on to the next chapter and explore "the process" of God's called and chosen.

CHAPTER SEVEN

THE PROCESS

We have already gone over some of the process that the disciples went through in some prior chapters, so let's pick up where Jesus begins to share with them what He is about to go through and what would ultimately take place. He tells them several different times, boldly, in the Books of Matthew, Mark, and Luke, and some just mere innuendos in the Book of John. But He does indeed tell them. Let's take a look at these accounts and see what we can garner from them. The very first time Jesus shares with them what is upcoming in His life and of His ultimate purpose for being on earth, is in Mark chapter 8. But before we get into that, we need to understand the setting.

The setting here is that after Jesus asks them who they thought He was, Peter confesses that Jesus is the Christ, the Son of the living God. Jesus teaches that Peter heard the voice of God for there was no way for him to know that, without the Spirit of the Father revealing it to him (in his mind) and Jesus then goes on to tell them the authority He would, in turn, give them because of that knowledge. He tells them that He'd give them the keys to the kingdom of heaven. He then commanded them not to tell anyone about it, not to tell anyone that He was indeed, Jesus the Christ. See, God had His process that must be adhered to. His Word does not come back to Him void. God already had many prophets proclaim to Israel what would happen to the Messiah, the Savior, in increments here and there. Then from that moment on, Jesus begins to share with them what was about to happen to Him. Let's look at Mark 8:31-33 – And He began to teach them that the Son of Man must suffer many things, and be rejected by the elders and chief priests and scribes, and be killed, and after three days rise again. He spoke this word openly. Then Peter took Him aside and began to rebuke Him. But when He had turned around and looked at His disciples, He rebuked Peter, saying, "Get behind Me, Satan! For you are not mindful of the things of God, but the things of men."

Let's break this down. First of all, Jesus rebuked Peter because He loved Peter. We know this because Jesus says to the lukewarm church in Revelation Chapter 3 verse 19, that as many as He loves, He rebukes and chastens. Secondly, we learn here that Peter listened to the lie of the enemy whispered to his mind, and Jesus didn't want that to be the beginning of a mindset of lies being built up in Peter's mind or in the other disciples' minds either, so He made sure that He cast that thought down in earshot of them all, that thought that exalted itself against the knowledge of God. He didn't want yet another mindset to be built up in the minds of any of His disciples. Thirdly, Jesus also spoke to Satan as well, out loud, so the disciples could hear and learn that the enemy never is mindful of the things of God, but the things of men, the things of this world that Satan is god of. They also needed to recognize that there would be two different types of voices that spoke to their minds.

Jesus foretold His death to His disciples the second time, in Luke 9. The setting for this one was right after the transfiguration which took place about a week after He told them the first time. Jesus had taken Peter, James, and John up to a mountaintop to pray and while Jesus was praying, His earthly appearance changed into His glorified form and His clothing became brilliantly, dazzling white. Moses and Elijah appeared with Jesus and they discussed His upcoming death and what it would signify, being Jesus' fulfillment of the Law (Moses) and the Prophets (Elijah). This sight frightened the disciples. Then God spoke after Peter wanted to build tents or booths, perhaps thinking of the festival of booths, showing either that perchance, he thought they were going to, or that he wanted to stay and dwell there. God spoke after a descending cloud overshadowed Jesus, Moses, and Elijah and He said, "This is My beloved Son in whom I am well pleased. Hear Him!" God wanted Jesus' inner circle of disciples to listen to what Jesus was teaching them. God showed them, at least a little bit of Jesus in His glorified state, knowing the Holy Spirit would bring it back to their remembrance when needed in the future. Their minds just could not comprehend all that Jesus was sharing with them at this point and time. In more modern terms, it just didn't compute. They fearfully fell on their faces at this and Jesus told them to get up and when they did, they only saw Jesus alone. He then instructed them to tell no one what they saw. Then, the faith growing encounter with the demon seized epileptic boy arose, accompanied by the lesson teaching them they needed to know God more personally, as we discussed in the last chapter.

Now that the setting has been laid out, let's turn to Luke 9:43-45 – And they were all amazed at the majesty of God. But while everyone marveled at all the things Jesus did, He said to His disciples, "Let these words sink down into your ears, for the Son of Man is about to be betrayed into the hands of men." But they did not understand this saying.... – Again, it just did not compute and was hidden from them. The third time Jesus told them of his impending death is found in Matthew 20. This time they were on their way to Jerusalem for Passover and Jesus explained to them that He would be mocked, scourged, crucified, and then rise again. But again, it did not compute and was hidden from them. Also, the more subtle forecasting of Jesus regarding His death, occur in John, chapters 12, 13, and 14 when Jesus corrects Judas about costly perfume being wasted on anointing Jesus rather than being sold to the poor. Jesus told them the woman needed to be left alone for she had saved it for anointing Him for the day of His burial and they would always have the poor with them, but not Him. Another place is when He tells the disciples that where He is going, they cannot come, and the third time where He talked about the giving of the Holy Spirit in His absence, hinting at His death and the future of the church. And again, they just did not compute.

I can completely understand all of this "not computing". During my 41 years of marriage to my husband, I know there are times when my brain glazed over not only because I didn't understand it, but because I really didn't want to hear about it since it just didn't compute. For example, I am a "words" kind of girl, not a "numbers" kind of girl, whereas my husband is a "numbers" kind of guy. He works in quality control, after all. So, when he starts explaining about numbers divided by numbers and thicknesses by fractions of numbers less than a human hair, I know my brain just checks out on him. He is also what some would call a "motorhead".

He used to race a dragster for years. So, when he tried to explain to me the differences in engines running on gasoline versus engines running on alcohol and the differences between regular motors and blower motors, and how transmissions and gears work, again, I know my brain just checked out. I couldn't understand it. It just did not compute and therefore, I just didn't want to hear about it because he had completely lost me.

I also know when I've spoken to him about a myriad of different things, his brain has checked out on me too. I could always see it in his eyes when he was not computing. For example, when I wanted to go shopping for the latest trends in clothing, explained seasonal colors, matching colors, prints and plains, thread counts, tailoring, softness versus pickiness on my skin, clothing and shoes breathing on hot humid days, etc. He was mentally gone; present, but not present. It just was not computing because in his mind, as long as his body, feet, and at times, his head were covered and protected, all was well with the world. And speaking of heads, he also could not compute the fact that I didn't like wearing hats because it messed up my hair. To him, hair is just hair, and your head needs to be protected from the elements in different seasons and weather. And, I'll just stop right there, as I'm sure you get the picture.

In getting back to the disciples and Jesus, the disciples would soon learn what Jesus was trying to teach them but was hidden now, with the upcoming events of Good Friday, Resurrection Sunday, and all that followed. Their understanding would be opened and then they would indeed compute. We know and focus on Jesus's Friday and Resurrection Sunday because they are the very base, the solid foundation of the good news of the gospel, but we don't often think too much about the fact that the disciples had that Friday to go through too. It was the very process God would utilize to bring them understanding and enlightenment, tearing down mindsets and strong-holds that had been built up within their minds. There was a lifechanging process that would take place between the two days for Jesus, and the disciples had a lifechanging process to go through as well.

See, that Friday, the disciples' hopes, dreams, and preconceived notions of what it meant to be followers of Jesus, what Jesus was preparing them for as His followers would be, look like, and entail, came to a screeching halt. Hadn't all of the people welcomed Jesus as the Messiah during His entry to the city, as an example? And therefore, on that Friday, they became disillusioned, confused, and depressed. In not comprehending what Jesus had been teaching as they filtered those experiences through the prism of their mindsets and human perspective, their carnal interpretation, they felt as though all was lost. They, therefore, couldn't grasp the fact that the mindsets that had been built up in their thinking about Jesus, themselves, and the kingdom of God needed to be torn down and that this was the beginning stage of that process. Every time Jesus taught them about His coming death, they didn't understand because the stronghold in their minds was that Jesus' coming kingdom was just around the corner and was to be one of historical magnificence with all of them holding positions of greatness and importance. This was a mindset stronghold that prevailed throughout Israel, especially in the minds of the Sadducees, Pharisees, scribes and teachers, the elite religious sect, believing this for themselves, and it had trickled down even to the common people. So that now, the disciples continued to believe the same thing, except with themselves, rather than the elite, holding those powerful positions. But they were afraid to ask Jesus about it, perhaps because they wanted and desired for His kingdom, the one they dreamed up and had mindsets about, to actually be just around the corner.

Let's take a peek at some of the things they said and did that give us glimpses into those preconceived notions, those mindsets. Right after Jesus healed the epileptic boy and foretold of His coming death, we find in Luke 9:46 that a dispute broke out among some of the disciples over which one of them would be the greatest. Jesus spoke to their wrong mindset by setting a little child before them and saying whoever is least among them will be the greatest. In Luke 9:54-56, we find James and John wanting to call down fire on a village that didn't receive Jesus as the Savior. He spoke to that mindset telling them they didn't know what spirit they were of and that He didn't come to destroy men's lives, but to save them.

Remember how the word instructs us to be renewed in the "spirit" of our minds.

We find another incident in Matthew 20:20-28. Here we find James and John even got their mother involved in their mindset. We find all three of them together with Mom asking if her two sons could sit on each side of Jesus in His kingdom. Jesus corrected this mindset by saying whoever desires to be first, let him be your slave just like He had come to serve and not be served. His kingdom would not have the same set up and structure that the Gentiles had in their kingdoms. Also, we find the disciples wanting to know when the end was and when Jesus would return for them to set up His kingdom. They wanted to know the sign of the times, things to look for when He was coming back. They clearly believed, had a mindset, that it would be in their lifetime. There are other examples revealing their wrong mindsets, but these relay the message quite nicely.

So yes, their Friday came to tear down their mindsets, turned strongholds. We all know the rest of the story with the resurrection of Jesus, bringing them to their own resurrection day in their understanding, His subsequent appearing to them, and of Pentecost where they received the baptism of the Holy Spirit, empowering them. It was through these experiences that the Holy Spirit brought back to their remembrance all the things Jesus taught them and the correct mindset was built up instead. That's when they began their ministries and began to change the world around them.

Now, let's take a look at the process of the Apostle Paul (his Roman name). First, let's look at a brief synopsis of his life gathered from the Scriptures to set the stage, so to speak, before His personal encounter with Jesus. He was born in Tarsus, which was a diverse community that highly valued education. He later moved to Jerusalem and was trained up under Gamaliel who was a Pharisee and an esteemed rabbi. Therefore, Paul was a zealous man of the Jewish faith. He did not believe Jesus was the Messiah, and thought Jesus was a heretic along with all of His followers of the "Way". Being taught in the Jewish faith meant that Paul knew the law of Leviticus 24:16 which states – "And whoever blasphemes the name of the LORD shall surely be put to death. All the congregation shall certainly stone him..." Blasphemy is basically insulting God's name by a mere man claiming to have the same attributes as God, or claiming a mere man did. Paul was all too eager to participate in stoning to death all those who followed the new faith Jesus brought, including Stephen. In Acts 26:9 ESV, we find Paul saying as much. "I myself was convinced that I ought to do many things in opposing the name of Jesus of Nazareth".

Paul had a wrong mindset built up from all of his teaching and training. He was totally, one hundred percent, convinced he was doing the right thing! He did not know and therefore did not believe that Jesus was the promised Messiah just as the Pharisees who taught him didn't. In other words, he believed the lies too. But he was called and chosen just as the other disciples were, so Jesus appeared to him to start his own process of tearing down his mindset, that stronghold set up in his mind, and then to rebuild it into one for God. As we know, while on his way to persecute more Christians, he had his Damascus Road encounter, or in other words, his Friday.

We find this in Acts 9:1-9 – Then Saul, (his name in Hebrew) still breathing threats and murder against the disciples of the Lord, went to the high priest and asked for letters from him to the synagogues of Damascus, so that if he found any who were of the Way, whether men or women, he might bring them bound to Jerusalem. As he journeyed, he came near Damascus, and suddenly a light shone around him from heaven. Then he fell to the ground, and heard a voice saying to him, "Saul, Saul, why are you persecuting Me?" And he said, "Who are You Lord?" Then the Lord said, "I am Jesus, whom you are persecuting. It is hard for you to kick against the goads." So, he, trembling and astonished, said, "Lord, what do You want me to do?" Then the Lord said, "Arise and go into the city, and you will be told what you must do." And the men who journeyed with him were speechless, hearing a voice but seeing no one. Then Saul arose from the ground and when his eyes were opened, he saw no one. But they led him by the hand and brought him into Damascus. And He was three days without sight, and neither ate nor drank.

We know on the third day, Ananias came to Paul after being instructed to by Jesus, and after laying hands on him, scales fell from Paul's eyes and he gained his sight and was baptized in the Holy Spirit. That third day was Paul's resurrection day just as the third day was Jesus' Resurrection Day, as well as the resurrection day of the disciples, so to speak. What's different with Paul, is that his process was now just beginning and it wasn't going to be easy in any way or by any means. Paul suffered a great deal right from the start as none of the disciples or others who were converted would believe him, let alone be anywhere near him. He had an uphill battle before him, for sure. But God had His process for Paul which turned into the miraculous just as it did with the disciples. And God has a process for each and every one of us. Let us rejoice and yield ourselves to the Holy Spirit of God as He works His process in each and every one of us, bringing us into maturity so He then can bring His church into the unity of faith in this new season, on this third and new day, to bring us into His miraculous!

In Acts 26:14-18, Paul explains about his mindset change to King Herod Agrippa II. It reads, "And when we all had fallen to the ground, I heard a voice speaking to me and saying in the Hebrew language, 'Saul, Saul. Why are you persecuting me? It is hard for you to kick against the goads.' So, I said, 'Who are You Lord?' And He said, 'I am Jesus, whom you are persecuting. But rise and stand on your feet; for I have appeared to you for this purpose, to make you a minister and witness both of the things which you have seen and of the things which I will yet reveal to you. I will deliver you from the Jewish people as well as from the Gentiles to whom I now send you, to open their eyes, in order to turn them from darkness to light, and from the power of Satan to God, that they may receive forgiveness of sins and an inheritance among those who are sanctified by faith in Me'"

Now, let's look at the phrase "kick against the goads". When farmers had yoked oxen pulling the plow to break up the fallow ground, the oxen were sometimes stubborn and didn't want to go. So, the farmers used goads which were long sticks with a pointed object on the ends like iron spikes, to get them going. The oxen didn't like being "goaded" and would kick back against the goad. It was futile though and quite painful, I'm sure, and most certainly made their lives harder than they had to be by just being obedient. In the King James Version, the word "pricks" is used in place of goads, and I like that too. Jesus told Paul it was hard to kick against them. He was informing Paul that he was living the hard life doing all that kicking back. As I was pondering over this, the Spirit led me to read Ecclesiastes 12. There in verse 11, it says, The words of the wise are like goads, and the words of scholars are like well-driven nails, given by one Shepherd. The ESV says it like this – The words of the wise are like goads and like nails firmly fixed are the collective sayings; they are given by one Shepherd.

When put all together, Jesus, our one Shepherd, was telling Paul he was kicking against the words the of the Christians he was persecuting, including Stephen whom he watched being stoned to death, and that those words he had heard them teaching time and time again, were indeed from God. The very God he claimed he was serving and killing in the name of. He should have listened to them and paid attention to his conscience being "pricked" with every word rather than staying yoked to the rabbis, priests, Sadducees and Pharisees. In so doing, he was choosing the hard life rather than choosing Jesus, the one Shepherd, who had taught in Matthew 11:28-30, "Come to Me, all you who labor and are heavy laden, and I will give you rest. Take my yoke upon you and learn from Me, for I am gentle and lowly in heart, and you will find rest for your souls. For My yoke is easy and My burden light."

Hallelujah! Thank you, Father God, for sending us Jesus, the answer to our every need, problem, and burden, and always ready to heal us of our wounds we got while kicking against Your pricks. Let us understand the process and be sensitive to Your voice, God, and not kick against the goads or pricks to our conscience as Paul did. May we allow Jesus to deliver us from our preconceived notions and our wrong mindsets that are a hard way of living, for they keep us yoked to the ways of the world! Thank you, Jesus! Amen!

CHAPTER EIGHT

THOUGHTS FUEL EMOTIONS

It is absolutely vital that we be aware of our thoughts and where those thoughts are leading us, for our thoughts fuel our emotions, whether those emotions are negative or positive. The Scriptures contain many examples of this for us to learn from, with the first examples found in the Book of Genesis. Genesis means the beginning or origin of something and I find that interesting in that Genesis not only explains the beginning of all creation, especially of the earth, but also of sin entering into mankind who was graciously given the responsibility of tending or caring for it, by God. Therefore, since sin is introduced in the beginning, it is of importance and something we need to pay close attention to for it is setting precedence on the nature of sin and the nature of the one who instigates it. We all know the first sin occurred in the garden of Eden with the devil interjecting thoughts into Eve's mind. She paid attention to the thought or question and pondered upon it, ultimately agreed with it, and then disobeyed God's instruction and sinned. Here we can glean how the enemy works from the very beginning. He is a thought interjector, he's a trouble maker, a pot stirrer, an instigator, and a liar. The enemy wants to plant lies in our minds that cause us to question who we are to and in God and who God is to us. He wants to shift our focus from God to ourselves and continue to beguile us down the path of separation from God into our ultimate destruction, if we should so choose to continue to follow his lead and don't cast his interjections down.

We also find our very first example of thoughts fueling emotions in the Book of Genesis with the very first offspring of mankind. It's the story of Cain and Abel, Adam and Eve's first two children. We find the account in chapter 4. Abel was a keeper of sheep and Cain was a tiller of the ground. Let's pick up the story in verses 3-7 – And in the process of time it came to pass that Cain brought an offering of the fruit of the ground to the LORD. Abel also brought the firstborn of his flock and of their fat. And the LORD respected Abel and his offering, but He did not respect Cain and his offering. And Cain was very angry, and his countenance fell. – At this point, some may be wondering why Cain's offering wasn't honored and we can find the answer to that in Jude 1:11 – ...For they have gone in the way of Cain, have run greedily in the error of Balaam for profit, and perished in the rebellion of Korah. – a brief overview of Balaam is that Balaam desired to curse the children of Israel for a price. If he cursed them, he would get paid handsomely for it. So, we learn that Cain brought some of the fruit he had cultivated, but not the best. He kept the best for himself, he wanted to profit from the best of his yield rather than offer it to God. We also learn that Cain was rebellious toward God and ultimately perished because of it just as Korah was rebellious toward God and did perish. Since we know that the enemy is a thought interjector, we can accept that the enemy interjected negative thoughts into the mind of Cain and he followed them as did his mother before him.

Now let's go back to the last line of verse 5. It says that Cain was very angry and his countenance fell. Allow me to break this down. Just from our own experiences in life, we can expect that Cain felt rejected by God and the enemy was right there to stir up that pot, and because Cain heeded the egging on of the devil, listening to his lies against God and his brother, that rejection then was fueled into jealousy of his brother and as he focused on that and allowed the enemy mind space, that jealousy received more fuel and grew into anger. Let's now continue to verses 6-7 – So the LORD said to Cain, "Why are you angry? And why has your countenance fallen?" We see here, that indeed, God is a discerner of our thoughts. Then God gives the antidote, so to speak, to Cain's listening to and following the interjections of the enemy. He says, in verse 7, "If you do well, will you not be accepted? And if you do not do well, sin lies at the door. And its desire is for you, but you should rule over it."

God was letting Cain know that he has a choice to make. He could rule over those high thoughts of the enemy, casting them aside and do well, or he could choose to not do well and allow the enemy's desire to take him down in sin, leading to self-destruction, and therefore, prevail over him. When we continue reading, we learn what Cain's choice was. We learn that he continued to kick against the goads. Verse 8 reads, Now Cain talked with Abel his brother; and it came to pass, when they were in the field, that Cain rose up against Abel his brother and killed him. In the above passage of Scriptures, we learn how the enemy operates if we allow him, if we give him a place in our minds, give him a foothold. The devil capitalized on the emotion of rejection, fueling it to grow into jealousy, and in not being dealt with, fueling that jealousy into anger and then to hatred, then ultimately fueling that hatred into murder. Note the process – from rejection to jealousy, to anger, to hatred, to murder.

We can also see the enemy try to utilize this strategy again, not in the exact order, but the same emotional elements. This time he is going to try and take down one of God's called, anointed, and chosen. This account is also found in Genesis and the story unfolds throughout several chapters. It is the story of Joseph and his brothers, with the main focus on his brothers. What we glean from the story is that Joseph is loved by Jacob his father more than all of his other children because Joseph was the son of his old age. Because Jacob favored Joseph, he made him a coat or tunic of many colors. When Joseph's older brothers saw that their father loved him more than all of them, they hated him. They hated Joseph so much that they couldn't even speak peaceably or kindly to him! That is intense emotion that has been fueled with the interjections of the enemy. Next, God gave little Joseph a dream showing through sheaves that all of Joseph's brothers bowed down before him. He shared it with his brothers and the Bible tells us that the brothers hated him even more because of his dreams and words. Then Joseph had yet another dream involving the sun, moon, and stars all bowing down to him. He again shared the dream with his brothers and then with his father, Jacob. The Scriptures say that his brothers envied Joseph and his father kept the matter in mind.

A little later, Jacob sends Joseph to go find his brothers who are out tending the sheep to make sure they are all doing well, and then return to him to give him the report of his brothers. While he is afar off on his way to his brothers, they recognized him, probably by way of his multi-colored tunic. Anyway, they began plotting and conspiring to kill him even before he reached them and came up with the story they would tell their father, that wild beasts had killed him. We can certainly see the enemy's strategy as he worked up Joseph's brothers from rejection, to hatred, to jealousy, and finally, to plotting murder. However, Joseph's brother Rueben did not kick against the goads as his brothers did, for he convinced his brothers not to kill Joseph, but to put him down into a pit with every intention of coming back, rescuing him, and returning him to their father. Anyway, when Joseph came up to them, his other brothers took his tunic from him and cast him into a waterless pit, then sat down to eat. While eating, they saw a caravan on their way to Egypt to sell wares. The brothers decided to prosper from their little brother rather than kill and shed blood and sold him to the caravan as a slave. When Rueben returned to the empty pit, he tore his clothes and reported to his brothers that Joseph was no more. So, they all conspired together and took Joseph's tunic, dipped it in goats' blood and returned it to their father who, in turn, assumed a wild beast had devoured Joseph and mourned. None of his sons or daughters were able to comfort him. Mind you, they could have if the brothers had told the truth, but they continued to allow their father to believe the lie. They continued to allow the devil a foothold, a place.

But as the Bible tells us that the devil is crafty, he devises other strategies and sometimes tries to lead us to self-destruction instead, like with Cain, by way of those thought interjections. As an example of this, the Lord has asked me to share an incident from my past that undoubtedly proves this to be true. When my thoughts got out of control, they just poured fuel onto the fire of my emotions and could have produced life altering results that would have been detrimental to the rest of my life. Those irrational thoughts, inspired by listening to the wrong voice egging me on, were causing my anger to grow up into stupidity and if it weren't for the Holy Spirit speaking the truth into my fired up thoughts and emotions roiling around in my mind, well, I just shudder to think of the end result and I praise His Holy name for rescuing me!

I was about fifteen or sixteen years old and living with my dad and adoptive mom. As I shared previously, my parents divorced when I was eight and a year later, I moved in with my dad and stepmom, and a year after that was adopted. My relationship with my adoptive mom wasn't a good one, tumultuous and rocky at best. She became abusive to me and there wasn't anything that would've or could've convinced me that she cared about me in the least little bit, nor any person, for that matter. Anyway, on this particular day, I overheard her on the phone with one of her friends while she was sitting at the kitchen table, once again lamenting on how rotten I was. I got angry and shouted at her to quit telling everyone I was a bad kid. I asked how come every other adult I knew, including my teachers and my friends' parents, praised me for being good, polite, and respectful, except for her? Now she became angry and let her friend go. Hanging up the receiver of the phone into its cradle on the wall, she stomped over to me huffing and puffing, and got up in my face as she went into a tirade right there in the middle of the kitchen.

She proceeded to tell me that yes, I was a good kid and it was all because of the way she raised me and rather than being ungrateful, I should show her some gratitude. She continued yelling that I was not out drinking like other teens my age because of her. I was not out there strung out on drugs like some teens my age because of her and the way she was raising me. She was really shouting and shaking now. She added, while mere inches from my face, that I was not another statistic of a pregnant teenager because of her, all the while, her spittle raining down all over my forehead and cheeks. I was incredulous! I was livid! I was fired up and furious, and as I was freeing my face of her spit, wiping it off with my hand, I, in disgust, blurted out, "You just keep on dreaming up stuff! I'm good because of the way my real mom and dad raised me from the day I was born, before we ever met you! And don't forget about Grama and Aunt Kay who also helped in my upbringing. How dare you try to take credit for what they did! They poured out unconditional love on me and not smackdowns, beatings, fat lips, welts, and bruises! Those things do not produce good kids!"

As she raised her hand up to belt me one, my dad shouted from the living room for both of us to knock it off! I ducked, then turned from her and marched into the living room and stood before my dad stretched out on the couch, eating from a bowl of ice-cream. I told him not to bother telling me to go to my room, for at this moment in time, there was no other place in the house I'd rather be and was going there on my own. I then turned and went down the hall to my room speed walking, stepped in, and then slammed the door shut behind me. I was fuming! I couldn't believe that my adoptive mom thought she was responsible for all of the things that my family taught me before I even came to live with her. As I was pacing back and forth alongside my bed, a memory popped up in my mind of when I had gone and spent the night with a girlfriend from school and when her mother brought me back home the following afternoon, she told my adoptive mom that I was welcome back anytime because I was a sweetheart, so polite, and a delight to be around. Then my adoptive mom said, right in front of my friend and her mother, "Yeah, well, you don't live with her!"

I then recalled how embarrassed and belittled I felt in that moment and started to pace even faster in my pent-up anger. Right then, I heard a voice in my head say, "You ought to show her! You should go out and get drunk, take some drugs, and get pregnant. Then she won't be able to say that anymore!"

"Yeah," I thought to myself! "That'll show her!"

Then the voice said, "You know tons of people you could call right now, and they would be more than happy to oblige you."

Immediately after, before I could listen to another dark thought, a different voice spoke in my mind and brought me to my senses. I recognized the voice as that of God as He spoke gently and soothingly, saying, "Don't. You are much too smart and too important to fall for that." And in that instant, it was like I was snapped out of a stupor. I then, shaking my head and with tears in my eyes, thanked Him as a peace settled around me. My anger was gone and I questioned in my mind how I ever could have even considered doing those things as it could have turned out disastrous and would have messed up the rest of my life. I then laid down on my bed, praising and thanking God in prayer, asking Him to forgive me for being so stupid, then drifted off to sleep…In thinking back on the whole thing, I am so thankful that I listened to the voice of the Holy Spirit and didn't kick against the goads, and responded positively to His prick. He brought me out of a blind rage. He is so good all the time! After that, it was so easy to understand what Paul was speaking about in Ephesians 4:26-27. He says, "Be angry and do not sin: do not let the sun go down on your wrath, nor give place to the devil." If we continue in anger and stew over the very reason we are mad, we are giving a place to the devil to stir up that anger, add fuel to it, and perhaps lead us to sin when we get up the next morning. It's best to focus on the good and let that negative emotion go before the day has ended.

The Bible also gives us examples of thoughts fueling emotions in a positive way. We can again, look to the story of Joseph. After he arrived in Egypt, he was sold by the caravan to Potiphar, an officer of Pharoah. The LORD was with Joseph and caused all that he did to prosper. Potiphar saw that the LORD was with him and bestowed favor on Joseph above his other slaves, and Joseph served Potiphar. Here we see that Joseph did not allow bitterness, or hatred to rule in his heart, that the interjections of the enemy into his mind did not take root. Because of this, Joseph became the overseer of his master's house with his master not knowing the goings on, the ins and outs of what he had, other than the blessings of the food put upon his table. He had no need to micro-manage Joseph for he could see that Joseph was faithful and capable, and prospered in all that he did.

The Scriptures tell us that Joseph was handsome and therefore, his master's wife wanted him. But Joseph refused her and told her that his master had committed everything in his house to him, except for her because she was his wife. He then questioned her as to how he could do this thing, a great wickedness and sin against God, and made his leave from her. Next, we can see that the interjector was messing with the wife's mind and she was heeding those thoughts, for she was after Joseph every day! But every day,

Joseph did not heed her to lie with her or even be around her. But then, the wife's evil plot fueled by the devil, came to fruition and when she saw Joseph alone in the house with no other servants around, she grabbed him by his garment and tried to seduce him again. But he ran outside leaving his garment in her hand. Then the interjector strikes again. The devil stirred up and fueled her emotions of rejection and anger of being spurned, into a plot of revenge. She called all of the other servants and lied saying Joseph tried to rape her and when she screamed in protest, he left in a hurry leaving his garment behind. When the master returned, she told the same lie and the master was angered and sent Joseph to prison.

While Joseph was in prison, we can conclude that the devil was still trying to mess with Joseph's mind because the Scriptures taught us how he works by injecting thoughts contrary to the Word of God. And we can conclude that Joseph rejected them all because God was still blessing and using him while in prison. He interpreted dreams of prisoners and was promised his name would be brought before the pharaoh, but never happened. Joseph didn't complain or get angry with God or the others who broke their promise, and not even his brothers who landed him in Egypt in the first place. He kept on trusting God for two whole years until the pharaoh himself had a dream that none of his wise men could interpret. It was then Joseph was remembered and brought before Pharoah. Joseph, by the leading of the Holy Spirit, was able to interpret the dream and prepare Egypt for the coming seven-year famine. Joesph was then made second in command over Egypt and God prospered Joseph. Joseph allowed his love of God and his faith in Him to fuel his emotions. He was grateful to God and continued moving in his servant's heart, never doubting God for a moment. Joseph then ultimately saved his entire family, including his brothers who had done him wrong. He held no grudge but operated in the love of God when his brothers came before him for help. This ultimately saved the whole Egyptian nation as well as Josephs' family bloodline.

Another example of thoughts fueling emotions in a positive way is, of course, in the life of Jesus, the children's bread. His is the most important example of all. He listened to no voice except that of

His Father God and made a way for saving every single tribe and tongue in the entire world if they would only heed and believe His words that are truth and freedom from the bondage of the enemy's lies and the ways of the world; the people who blindly incorporate them. Jesus went through rejection, betrayal, hatred, and physical abuse and yet, through it all, He never stopped loving nor living in compassion.

The first of four examples that truly impress me is when Jesus looked upon Jerusalem, who had rejected and hated Him, and would ultimately crucify Him, with such love. It's found in Matthew 23:37-39. "Oh Jerusalem, Jerusalem, the one who kills the prophets and stones those who are sent to her! How often I wanted to gather your children together, as a hen gathers her chicks under her wings, but you were not willing! See! Your house is left to you desolate; for I say to you, you shall see Me no more till you say, 'Blessed is He who comes in the name of the LORD!'"

The second example is when Jesus literally weeps as He looks upon Jerusalem and is found in Luke 19:41-44. – Now as He (Jesus) drew near, He saw the city and wept over it, saying, "If you had known, even you, especially in this your day, the things that make for your peace! But now they are hidden from your eyes. For days will come upon you when your enemies will build an embankment around you, surround you, and close you in on every side. And level you, and your children within you to the ground; and they will not leave in you one stone upon another, because you did not know the time of your visitation."

The third is when Jesus' dear friend Lazurus dies and again, Jesus wept. This is found in John chapter 11. It tells us what happens when Mary, one of Lazurus' sisters came to Him. Verses 32-36 read – Then, when Mary came where Jesus was, and saw Him, she fell down at His feet, saying to Him, "Lord, if You had been here, my brother would not have died." Therefore, when Jesus saw her weeping, and the Jews who came with her weeping, He groaned in the spirit and was troubled. And He said, "Where have they laid him?" They said to Him, "Lord, come and see." Jesus wept. Then the Jews said, "See how He loved him!" – I believe He wept when He saw Mary and the people who came with her weeping because it is at this point the Scripture says Jesus was troubled and groaned within His spirit. This shows that He had compassion on the people and hurt because they were hurting deeply. Then Jesus wept even though He knew Lazurus was not gone for good because He was about to raise him up from the dead.

The fourth example is when Jesus was hanging on the cross, and cried out to God to forgive the people who had wrangled to have Him crucified and jeered at him as He was slowly dying. In Luke 23:24, Jesus prays for them as His very life was waning from Him. He said, "Father, forgive them, for they do not know what they do." What love, what compassion! Jesus was able to come to this place for He listened to the voice of the Father, and His voice alone. And this is the very place that God is calling for His saints to be in this new visitation upon the earth, now.

We have learned that the mind is a hunting ground for the enemy. You can have one tiny thought that is not from God, and the devil, our adversary, will run with it, trying to get you to get yourself by listening to his lies and acting upon them, turning those negative thoughts into negative emotions that you could carry in your heart for decades, or lead you to do something you will regret later if you don't cast those interjected thoughts down in the name of Jesus! Renewing the mind via the word of God is foundational to us growing, maturing, changing, and digging up those roots of rejection, jealousy, anger, hatred, bitterness, and the like, so God can transform our minds and thereby transform us.

I pray that God would be with us, and lead us to come to maturity and be able to put down the hatred and division that so besets our society today and walk in the path that Jesus did. Oh, Lord, help us to have ears to listen and respond to only your Spirit and not the interjections of the enemy and to have eyes to see from your kingdom perspective. I ask this in the precious name of Jesus. Amen!

CHAPTER NINE

SOUND MIND

Once the Holy Spirit began showing me how important our minds and the thoughts that we think are, as well as our thought processes, I was amazed at how many verses in the Scriptures are written about that very thing. They just began popping off the pages of my Bible as I read and studied it. Not just the words minds, and think, and thoughts, but all of the synonyms for them as well. They include consider, choose, perceive, think, meditate, understand, remember, judge, believe, discern, know, plan, ponder, reason, acknowledge, imagine, deceive, suppose, contemplate, and many more as well, but I'm sure you are getting the gist of it. And in seeing these throughout the Scriptures in both the Old Testament and the New, we can understand to an even greater degree, just how vitally important it is for us to pay attention to our thoughts and guard our minds.

Some of the verses I read were Isaiah 26:3 – You will keep him in perfect peace, whose mind is stayed on you... Proverbs 16:3 – Commit your works to the Lord, and your thoughts will be established, Psalm 4:4 – Be angry, and do not sin. Meditate within your heart on your bed, and be still, Hebrews 3:1 NIV – ...Fix your thoughts on Jesus, Psalm 7:9 – Oh, let the wickedness of the wicked come to an end, But establish the just; For the righteous God tests the hearts and minds. Philippians 4:7 – and the peace of God, which surpasses all understanding, will guard your hearts and minds through Christ Jesus, Proverbs 14:30 MSG – A sound mind makes for a robust body but runaway emotions corrode the bones. As I read that last verse, I was reminded of 2 Timothy 1:7 – For God has not given us a spirit of fear, but of power and of love and of a sound mind. Then for days I kept hearing the Holy Spirit speak to me those two words, sound mind, sound mind, sound mind. And then, I suddenly knew the Lord wanted me to focus on "sound mind" and therefore, I went into research mode.

What I first discovered was that Timothy was pastor over the church in Ephesus when Nero was the emperor, in charge of the Roman Empire. Nero was known for hunting down Christians and tormenting and torturing them to death by the most vile, gruesome, insane, and evil ways. Nero had what I'll call a squad of "Christian hunters" who "sniffed out" any and all Christians (much like our police drug and explosive sniffing dogs today) so as to put them to death for Nero's own sick, evil, delight and entertainment. Therefore, Timothy probably fearfully supposed Nero would take extreme pleasure in capturing and torturing him to death, considering him a prime target and catch, as he was a pastor over many and in shepherding them, he would have to give an account for them. At this time, Paul, his mentor and spiritual father, had been imprisoned and Timothy probably felt all alone and just out there as a beacon flag waving in the wind or an X marks the spot on a treasure map. So, Paul wrote Timothy a letter from prison, and in it, told him to remember that God has not given us a spirit of fear, but one of power, love, and a sound mind.

Now that the scene has been set, let's delve deeper into the words sound mind. I absolutely love what my research yielded and I'm sure you will too. I looked up the words sound mind in the original Greek that they were written in and found that in the Greek, sound mind is actually a compound word and since in our English language, there was no comparable word for it, it was translated into two words. The compound word in the Greek language is sophroneo, combining two Greek words sodzo and phroneo. The Greek word sodzo means to be saved or delivered. It suggests something that has been set free, liberated, revitalized, restored, reestablished, recovered, and protected, so hence, is now safe and secure. The second part of the phrase "sound mind" is phroneo which carries the idea of a person's intellect or total frame of mind, thinking that encompasses one's rationale or reasoning, logic, and emotions. It refers to every part of the human mind including all of the processes that are engaged in making the mind function and come to conclusions, and it also implies thoughts that are cherished and a mental habit.

When the words sodzo and phroneo are compounded into just one word, they again, form the word sophroneo which illustrates a mind that has been delivered, protected, rescued, revived, revitalized, salvaged, and is now safe and secure in God. Thus, even if our mind is tempted to succumb to fear, as was the case with Timothy, we can allow God's word, our bread, Christ Jesus, and the Holy Spirit to work in us to deliver, rescue, revive, and salvage our minds. This means our rationale or reasoning, logic, and emotions can be shielded from the illogically, absurd, ridiculous, unfounded, and crazy thoughts that have tried to grip our minds in the past and try to creep in during the present as well. All we have to do is grab hold of and hang on tightly to God's word, our Christ Jesus, and His Holy Spirit, to cherish them all and allow them to become our mental habit.

While putting this all together, I was reminded of several Scripture passages being composed together, ones that we have already touched on in whole or in part in prior chapters, that really highlight the above process. They are 2 Corinthians 10:4-5 – "For the weapons of our warfare are not carnal but mighty in God for pulling down strongholds, casting down arguments and every high thing that exalts itself against the knowledge of God, bringing every thought into captivity to the obedience of Christ". And Romans 12:2 "And do not be conformed to this world, but be transformed by the renewing of your mind, that you may prove what is that good and acceptable and perfect will of God.". As well as Ephesians 4:17-24 – This I say, therefore, and testify that you should no longer walk as the rest of the Gentiles walk, in the futility of their mind, having their understanding darkened, being alienated from the life of God, because of the ignorance that is in them, because of the blindness of their heart; who, being past feeling, have given themselves over to lewdness, to work all uncleanness with greediness. But you have not so learned Christ, if indeed you have heard Him and have been taught by Him, as the truth is in Jesus: that you put off, concerning your former conduct, the old man which grows corrupt according to the deceitful lusts, and be renewed in the spirit of your mind, and that you put on the new man which was created according to God, in true righteousness and holiness. Also, Philippians 4:6-8 – Be anxious for nothing, but in everything by prayer and supplication, with thanksgiving, let your requests be known onto God; and the peace of God, which surpasses all understanding, will guard your hearts and minds through Christ Jesus. Finally, brethren, whatever things are noble, whatever things are just, whatever things are pure, whatever things are lovely, whatever things are of a good report, if there is anything praiseworthy – meditate on these things.

All along in the above-mentioned Scripture passages, Paul was teaching on how to have a sound mind, and seeing all of this throughout the different Scriptures in the New Testament was just mind-blowing to me! Furthermore, as I contemplated on all of this, the Holy Spirit drew my attention to the fact that Jesus, when He first started His ministry publicly, was telling everybody to change their minds from what they had previously been taught and believed to be true. Let's take a look at Matthew 4:17. It reads – From that time (after being tempted in the wilderness) Jesus began to preach and to say, "Repent, for the kingdom of heaven is at hand." As we discussed earlier, repent is the Greek word metanoeo and it generally means to change one's mind. Here though, let's dig a little deeper. To repent is more than a logical or religious recognition that a person must change their mind. To repent is to respond to that inner, or in other words, that spiritual perception of the necessity to make a decision to change the direction of one's life and then, to do so.

As I was marveling over this, the Holy Spirit spoke to me yet again, saying, if you think that is marvelous, turn back over to Eve being tempted in the Garden of Eden and read it again, and so I did. Genesis 3:1-6 teaches – Now the serpent was more cunning than any beast of the field which the LORD God had made. (This tells us the serpent was made by God) And he said to the woman, "Has God indeed said, "You shall not eat of every tree in the garden'?" And the woman said, "We may eat the fruit of the trees in the garden; but of the fruit of the tree in the midst of the garden, God has said, 'You shall not eat it lest you die.'" Then the serpent said to the woman, "You will not surely die. For God knows that in the day you eat of it your eyes will be opened, and you will be like God, knowing good and evil." So, when the woman saw that the tree was good for food, that it was pleasant to the eyes, and a tree desirable to make one wise, she took of its fruit and ate…"

It was at this point the Holy Spirit spoke again. He said, "Do you see that? The devil was challenging Eve's thought processes, the way she thought about what God had told her. He was tempting her to perceive what God had spoken differently, to change her mind and turn. She listened to and considered the interjected thought and, therefore, did indeed change her mind about what God had told her. She now distrusted Him and His word, and thereby acted upon her changed thought processes that caused her to have a changed mind. So then, seeing the fruit differently than previously, she acted upon her changed mind, disobeyed, and partook of the forbidden." Wow! I knew in that moment that the Holy Spirit was showing me that the purpose of the enemy interjecting thoughts into our mind, as we discussed in the previous chapter, is for the ultimate goal of getting us to change our mind about the Word of God, the truth, and our trust in it, the way we perceive it, to lead us astray. And as I pondered more upon this, I came to the understanding that everything, every single thing, begins with a thought, whether good or evil, and it's our responsibility on how we respond to that initial thought, the path we allow it to take in our minds, which in turn, causes us to act, in one way or the other. Our mind is indeed a battlefield with pricks or goads of truth from the Holy Spirit battling against the fiery darts of lies from the wicked one.

As I reflected on the things the Holy Spirit showed me concerning the mind, I began to think about not just the psychological aspects, but the physiological aspects too, not just the thought processes, but the physical makeup of the brain, the natural organ that God created all mankind with. As I did this, I recalled hearing snippets, bits and pieces, of scientific studies and reports on the news over the last couple of decades. I recalled hearing that scientific studies had shown that people of faith who spent a lot of time in prayer were proven to be happier people. (I remember thinking, "I could have told you that.") And another that proved that positive thinking and prayer literally boosted our immune system's ability to ward off disease as well as heal us from some of them.

Anyway, the latest one I heard was just last week and was a study on military veterans showing that those vets who suffered stress and PTSD had developed psoriasis on their skin, while those vets who weren't stressed out about their service time, had no psoriasis.

When I heard that on the news, I remembered a conversation I had with my allergist after suffering allergic reactions to many antibiotics and other medications. My allergist told me to not take the red, raised, itchy, burning skin and/or hives, lightly. He explained they were serious because our skin is an organ of the body, the largest organ actually, and is on the outside of our body. He continued saying because it is on the outside, we can see the effects of the reaction. He then told me to just imagine the havoc that was being wreaked on my inside organs that we couldn't see, explaining that if something effects one organ, it affects them all. Yes, even our heart, brain, lungs, liver, and the like. So, we can conclude that when our brains are being affected, it also has an effect on our other organs too, including the skin, whether good or bad and that our inside turmoil definitely can wreak havoc both inside and outside of our bodies.

After putting these two things together, especially remembering the brain, the Lord brought back to my memory of when I was in medical school and was learning about the brain. I remember how I loved my teacher, whom we called Mrs. C. I loved how she taught, as she was a Christian and taught our lessons including her Biblical perspective of some of them alongside the science. I remember studying about the neurotransmitter, dopamine, and how it is crucial for balanced thought and emotion. It helps with focus and staying on task. It also supports the brain's ability to recall life's significant moments, whether wonderful or tragic. We learned that a balanced arrangement of neural chemistry and circuitry in the brain resulted in astonishingly creative and deeply religious people and these people of faith, by way of prayer and meditation on God's Word, literally boosted the activity of their dopamine. This neurotransmitter is also referred to as the "chemical of more" because you always want more of it since it makes you feel so good.

Dopamine is also involved with motivation for seeking a good reward. (I'm reminded here, of how often the Scriptures speak of good rewards in heaven. Thank you, Jesus!) Dopamine is also involved with our memory, our moods, and our attention. The dopamine control center encompasses our judgement, planning, impulse control, and our continuing happiness. It helps us to think before we act, therefore helps stop unhealthy behaviors. In order to have continuing happiness, our dopamine levels need to be balanced because too much or too little of it causes us problems. As an example, too much dopamine has been tied to obsession, agitation, compulsiveness, psychosis, and violence. I remember a study where scientists by way of various brain scans discovered that out of one hundred convicted murderers, about half of them committed their crimes while they were hopped up on methamphetamines which raise the dopamine levels in our brains.

Speaking of which, what was astounding to me was learning the fact that all drug and alcohol abuse actually come from the craving of more dopamine, but rather than allowing it to occur naturally by way of prayer, meditation, and/or physical activity like swimming, running, biking, etc., they opt for and get addicted to the artificial dopamine stimulators that more often than not, produce too much. Then the users go from a feeling of happiness or euphoria to depression and agitation as they come down from the high and into low levels of dopamine. Low levels of dopamine can cause depression, low motivation, apathy, boredom, fatigue, sugar cravings, disbelief, skepticism, and even Parkinson's disease. It has been associated with short attention spans, distractibility, disorganization, procrastination, and even linked to thrill seekers and to those who love to argue and are always looking to create or stir up conflict. Then sadly, when the addict's dopamine levels crash down as their artificial stimulant wears off, they use more. This creates that unhealthy cycle of causing their brain to continuously go on an up and down rotation while using their drug of choice. What's especially bad about those artificial dopamine stimulators is that they become less and less effective with each use and therefore, the addicts use more and more of it causing that vicious cycle of addiction highs and lows that can eventually lead to death.

I also remember learning about our thalamus. It's a portion of brain matter near the center of our brains. One of its primary functions is to help us identify what is real and what isn't. Every feeling, sensation, and thought process passes through our thalamus as it goes to other parts of our brain. I remember learning that if the thalamus stopped functioning, we would be essentially comatose. I also remember Mrs. C teaching that the more we think about something, the more active our thalamus becomes and will eventually begin to respond to that something as though it were real. She said she believed that the more someone focuses on God, the more real He becomes to them and she wondered if God gave us the gift of faith through our thalamus. The Scripture tells us to draw near to God, and He will draw near to us. She believed the opposite was true too, that if someone doesn't think about or contemplate on God, the less real He becomes to them and any faith one may have had, dwindles away. Perhaps that is why Paul said to stir up the gift that is within you. Also, on the other hand, this is the route taken in brains when people "believe" the lie that the Scriptures talk about. They focus so much on it, that the lie becomes real, "their truth". As a matter of fact, this perfectly explains why the devil wants to constantly assault our minds with his lies! The more we listen and focus on them, the more real those lies are to us and become a mindset and then a stronghold in our mind, just like the lie I believed, that I was unlovable when I was a just a kid, that became a stronghold in my life. This also explains how Paul believed wholeheartedly that he was doing the right thing in persecuting all of the followers of Jesus and His "Way". He focused so much on it, that it actually became real to him in his mind!

As I reflected on all of the above, it was clear to me that our minds and our bodies are in constant communication with each other. Our minds and our thoughts are extremely potent and powerful to the point that our thoughts literally, physically, change pathways in our brains and the firing of brain chemicals. I'm thinking that is what Paul was speaking about when he said all of the above-mentioned Scripture verses concerning our minds and where to focus them. Go back and re-read them for a moment and see the connections between them and the science just discussed.

I'm also thinking that since our brain is always communicating with our bodies, it has the ability to change our bodies too, and therefore our thought processes and beliefs, the things we focus on, can literally create both mental and physical illness or disease, or eradicate them. As a matter of fact, if we look again at the Scripture verse Proverbs 14:30 MSG – A sound mind makes for a robust body but runaway emotions corrode the bones, it basically says just that. This is just mind blowing to me!

Along the same lines, as I re-read 2 Corinthians 10:4-5 For the weapons of our warfare are not carnal but mighty in God for pulling down strongholds, casting down arguments and every high thing that exalts itself against the knowledge of God, bringing every thought into captivity to the obedience of Christ, my eyes focused on the word captivity. I then saw in my mind's eye, those high thoughts like cattle running around wildly in a field – the mind – then cowboys herding them all into the corral, holding them captive in it as they shut the gate when all were rounded up. The field was free of the wild beasts now and beautiful flowers began to sprout up and grow in the field, the flowers representing the pure, lovely, noble, virtuous and good thoughts we're instructed to think on. It amazed me the way our mind and brain function when we do as Scripture teaches us, that our thoughts then actually, literally, bring about deliverance from mental and physical disease and inflictions that were previously created through our wrong thought processes. God created our brains and how they function so that when our brains are working in a healthy Scriptural way, after we accept salvation and are both water and Spirit baptized, we receive deliverance, and our minds are liberated, revitalized, restored, reestablished, recovered, salvaged, and protected, so hence, are now safe and secure! Just wow!

As I was reflecting on all of the medical science and how our brains physically change with our thoughts, even down to the cellular level, I wondered if our genes were then affected too, so I went into research mode again. And sure enough, I found some recent research done on it. As we know, our genes carry directions for every aspect of our physical and psychological make up. In a nutshell, some of the key findings of these scientists suggest that that too much stress related thinking speeds up cellular aging, which can make us more susceptible to illness and disease. In other words, negative and pessimistic thought patterns that persist for years can damage our DNA by damaging the telomeres which are the protective tips of our DNA molecules, or in other words, our chromosomes. Our chromosomes that our children inherit from us. Also, on the flip side, long periods of positive thinking and meditation or prayer, change our genes too. Interestingly, some of the changes were observed in our genes that are the current specific targets of anti-inflammatory and analgesic drugs. Others were the targets of medications used in treating a myriad of mental dysfunctions like depression and bipolar disorder. After discovering all of this, I thought of how we inherit genes from our parents, and they, from their parents and so on. In other words, genes are passed down on to generation upon generation.

At this point, I remembered that the Bible spoke of generations in many Scriptures, but the ones that blew me away were from Deuteronomy 5:9 – …For I, the LORD your God, am a jealous God, visiting the iniquity of the fathers upon the children to the **third and fourth generations** of those who hate Me. And Deuteronomy 7:9 – Therefore know that the LORD your God, He is God, the faithful God who keeps covenant and mercy for a thousand generations with those who love Him and **keep His commandments**. (Emphasis mine) And from Psalm 78:4-6 – And we will not hide them from their children, telling to the generation to come the praises of the LORD, and His strength and His wonderful works that He has done. For He established a testimony in Jacob, and appointed a law in Israel, which commanded our fathers that they should make them known to their children; that the generation to come might know them, the children who would be born, that they may arise and declare them to their children. – All of the above Scriptures speak indirectly of our genes and genetics, whether good or bad, that are passed down through our DNA to the generations after us and from the generations before us that we inherited our genes from. And what we focus on in our thoughts, literally alters our DNA, so that even though our parents before us may not have served God, all we have to do is exactly what God told Cain. Do well, and you will be accepted by Him, but if you don't, sin lies in wait for you, just rule over it! That's all. Just do well, being lovingly obedient to His every word in the Scriptures. Again, just Wow!

I am literally astounded that what science is now discovering and has discovered in the recent past, God has said all along through His Holy Scriptures in both the Old and the New Testaments. In essence, by doing what God and Jesus direct us to do in meditating on His Word, praying to Him often; spending one-on-one personal time with Him, and allowing Him to transform our minds into the mind of Christ, giving us that sound mind, it literally, physically brings deliverance to us from many of the disorders, ailments, diseases and some addictions we have suffered from and also can protect us from developing them in the first place! And then as we raise our children, the next generation, up in the Word of God, that deliverance is theirs and so on, to many generations by way of genetics! Truly, Jesus, our bread of life, the children's bread, is deliverance!

I have always known and shared that God is, for lack of a better term, awesome, however, He blows my mind and delights my soul when He continues to show me how much more awesome He is; more awesome than I could ever think or imagine. I praise Him for that and pray He does the same for you, in Jesus' name, Amen!!

CHAPTER TEN

BEWARE OF THE BABYLON MINDSET

As I was considering everything the Lord had shown me for this book thus far, I thought of Babylon falling in the end, as recorded in the Book of Revelation, and as I pondered on that, the Spirit of the Lord asked me to go back and read about all three of the Babylons beginning with the tower of Babel back in Genesis, the book of beginnings. This account takes place after the flood. Chapter 11:1-9 tells the story, and we can also glean some more information about it from other Scripture. Let's take a look at the story – Now the whole earth had one language and one speech. And it came to pass, as they journeyed from the East, that they found a plain in the land Shinar, and they dwelt there. Then they said to one another, "Come, let us make bricks and bake them thoroughly." They had brick and asphalt for mortar. And they said, "Come, let us build ourselves a city, and a tower whose top is in the heavens; let us make a name for ourselves, lest we be scattered abroad over the face of the whole earth."

But the LORD came down to see the city and the tower which the sons of men had built. And the LORD said, "Indeed the people are one and they all have one language, and this is what they begin to do; now nothing that they propose to do will be withheld from them. Come let Us go down and there and confuse their language, that they may not understand one another's speech." So, the LORD scattered them abroad from there over the face of all the earth, and they ceased building the city. Therefore, its name is called Babel, because there the LORD confused the language of all the earth; and from there the LORD scattered them abroad over the face of the earth. Other Scripture tells us that it was Nimrod, the great grandson of Noah, who built the city.

Let's look at Genesis 10:8-11 – Cush begot Nimrod; he began to be a mighty one on the earth. He was a mighty hunter before the LORD; therefore, it is said, "Like Nimrod the mighty hunter before the LORD." And the beginning of his kingdom was Babel, Erech, Accad, and Calneh, in the land of Shinar. From that land he went to Assyria and built Ninevah… Nimrod is also mentioned in Micah 5:6 – They shall waste with the sword the land of Assyria, and the land of Nimrod at its entrances; Thus, He shall deliver us from the Assyrian, when he comes into our land and when he treads within our borders.

What we gather from these verses is again, that Nimrod was the great grandson of Noah, and he is the one who built the city of Babel, among other cities that at one point or another rebelled against God, and is most likely the one who gave the instructions to build the tower within Babel. As I studied these things, the Lord reminded me that His instructions to Noah and his sons after He blessed them was to be fruitful and multiply, and fill the earth in Genesis 9:1. However, the people rebelled against God, gathered in one place, started to build a tower to reach into heaven (God's domain) to exalt themselves above God's word to them, and even said blatantly, let's make a name for ourselves unless we be scattered over the whole face of the earth. This was total defiance against what God instructed them to do. The Holy Spirit also brought to my attention that this was post-flood and God had already vowed to never destroy the earth again by water. But here, mankind was once more doing evil and disobeying Him. He wasn't going to let all of mankind descend into complete depravity again so soon, so His plan this time was to stop their wickedness by turning their one common language into many and this ultimately caused them to obey His word. They were scattered over the face of the earth after God confused their language into many, so that they had to get together in groups they could understand and move out in those groups. Hallelujah!

I just love God! He is so smart and wise, and always has a plan for His will to be done in the earth as it is in heaven! Just like He did with Jonah when he disobeyed God and started sailing away in the opposite direction God had told him to go. God sent a big fish that swallowed him and brought him to Ninevah, right where God said he was to go! God most definitely moves in the affairs of, and in the midst of men, despite their disobedience to Him. Thank you, Father! God also brought to my attention that the people were seeking the very thing Eve did after being tempted and ultimately succumbed to the temptation of the enemy in the garden. We can just see the same strategy the enemy used. We can almost hear the interjections of the devil – You don't need God, you can be your own God, be just as smart as He is. Be the God of your own life! All you have do is (insert the enemy's wicked plan that best fits the situation) and exalt yourself to His level. We see that the devil's strategy had not changed.

Next, let's take a look hundreds of years later at Babylon. We'll look at a brief synopsis of what occurred in the Book of Daniel. King Nebuchadnezzar was on top of the world with the most formidable army the world had ever seen. Therefore, he prided himself of his own magnificence, prowess, brilliance, and cleverness as well as his power over the Israelites that he had conquered and brought back to Babylon as slaves. What he didn't realize is that it was God who gave him that power using him to bring judgement upon His people because of their disobedience. Because of the king's pompous thoughts and ways, taking credit himself for what God had done, he would be brought low, for it is indeed God who rules in the midst of men and sets in power whom He chooses, for His own good purposes. God let him know, through a series of dreams interpreted by Daniel, what would happen to the one who refused to acknowledge God. But yet, King Nebuchadnezzar insisted it was he himself who had brought Babylon to its greatness by speaking, asking is not this great Babylon, that I have built for a royal dwelling by my mighty power and for the honor of my majesty? Oh-oh, bad choice! We can very clearly see that the king had been listening to the interjections of the enemy, to not need nor heed God, because he could be just like God and self-command his own life, and be the master of his own destiny and live in his own power, the very same thing Eve was tempted with back in the garden.

Next, because of that bad choice, King Nebuchadnezzar became insane and had the mind of an animal and thus lived like one for seven years as Daniel had told him would happen if he didn't humble himself and acknowledge God had given him that kingdom. After those seven years were up, just as Daniel had told him, his understanding returned to him and he reverted back to his old self, but blessed God. All his earthly blessings, including his royal staff, that he had previously enjoyed were restored to him and he quickly returned to his former place of majesty with one great exception, he now was ready to sing the praises of God Most High, as he understood the truth rather than the enemy's whispered lies of self-importance, pride, and independent sovereignty. King Nebuchadnezzar declared the truth this time, proclaiming, "Now I, Nebuchadnezzar, praise and extol and honor the King of heaven, all of whose works are truth, and His ways justice. And those who walk in pride He is able to put down." So here, we see the enemy's same strategy again and that it had not changed. Notice the pattern. We do see a different outcome here however, and that is one of humility and acknowledgement of God and all of His powerful attributes and majesty, not the king's own. That same choice lies in each and every one of us, and will until the end of days.

And speaking of the end of days, let's now take a look at the Babylon found in the Book of Revelation. First, Revelation 17 gives us a hint regarding it. Verses 4-6 are John explaining what he saw in the Spirit. – The woman was arrayed in purple and scarlet, and adorned with gold and precious stones and pearls. Having in her hand a golden cup full of abominations and filthiness of her fornication. And on her forehead a name was written: MYSTERY, BABYLON THE GREAT, THE MOTHER OF HARLOTS AND OF THE ABOMINATIONS OF THE EARTH. I saw the woman drunk with the blood of the saints and with the blood of the martyrs of Jesus. And when I saw her, I marveled with great amazement. Next, let's look at chapter 18:1-3 – After these things I saw another angel coming down from heaven, having great authority, and the earth was illuminated with his glory. And he cried mightily with a loud voice, saying, "Babylon the great is fallen, is fallen, and has become a dwelling place of demons. A prison for every foul spirit, and a cage for every unclean and hunted bird! For all the nations have drunk of the wine of the wrath of her fornication, the kings of the earth have committed fornication with her, and the merchants of the earth have become rich through the abundance of her luxury."

Also, let's look at verses 9-11 and then 15-16, and then verse 20 – This is still the angel speaking, "The kings of the earth who committed fornication and lived luxuriously with her will weep and lament for her, when they see the smoke of her burning, standing at a distance for fear of her torment, saying, 'Alas, alas that great city Babylon, that mighty city! For in one hour your judgment has come.' And the merchants of the earth will weep and mourn over her, for no one buys their merchandise anymore". Verse 15-16 – "The merchants of these things, who became rich by her, will stand at a distance for fear of her torment, weeping and wailing, and saying, 'Alas, alas, that great city that was clothed in fine linen, purple, and scarlet, and adorned with gold and precious pearls!'" And finally, at verse 20 – "Rejoice over her, O heaven, and you holy apostles and prophets, for God has avenged you on her!" – Again, we see that the devil's strategy had not changed. However, this time we find there is no repentance as with King Nebuchadnezzar, but the people who built these systems under the influence of the enemy, actually got mad at God and blasphemed Him in Chapter 16:21! It's reminiscent of Job 15:25 – For he stretches out his hand against God, and acts defiantly against the Almighty –Yikes! But their eternal demise is eminent. Now, let's unpack all of this.

As I was reading chapters 17 and 18 of Revelation, I heard the Spirit of the Lord speak to me telling me that the spiritual Babylon of Revelation is being built and strengthened right now, in this age, and although the enemy is moving differently in our day, moving in large systems, i.e., the political, economic, and religious systems, doesn't mean the devil has left us alone and no longer is bringing individual temptations. It doesn't mean that now, we as individuals, are no longer important and are just peons to him because the enemy presently has bigger fish to fry, as some well-known ministers have proclaimed in the not-too-distant past. And just as alarming, many churches don't teach or speak about the devil at all. However, Paul states that we are not ignorant of Satan's devices, nevertheless, if we're not taught them through the

Scriptures, then unfortunately, we are. Believing that we Christians are of little or no significance to the god of this world is a very slippery slope. The Scriptures clearly teach in 1 Peter 4:8 that we are to be sober and vigilant because our adversary the devil walks about as a roaring lion, seeking "whom" he may devour. Know that the above-mentioned spiritual systems are perpetuated and adhered to by many individual "whoms", and the devil most assuredly is there in it, one way or the other, directly or indirectly.

Once again, we can turn back to Genesis 3 and the Garden of Eden to see what the Holy Spirit is teaching. There we see that the serpent deceived Eve as we previously discussed. But you know what you won't find in there? You won't read that the serpent tempted or deceived Adam. He didn't need to because Eve was right there to do it for him. Verse 6 says…She also gave to her husband with her, and he ate. Just like that, he ate. Also, Paul said to the Corinthians, in 2 Corinthians 11:3 – But I fear, lest somehow, as the serpent deceived Eve by his craftiness, so your minds may be corrupted from the simplicity that is in Christ. Notice Paul said Eve, not Adam and Eve. I often wondered why Adam didn't correct Eve with what God had said. Well, Eve is the woman God gave him as his helper suitable for him after saying it wasn't good for him to be alone. Therefore, she had great influence in his life. When God later questioned him about why he ate of the tree, Adam told God that the woman whom He had given her, gave it to him and so he ate, confirming the influence she had with him.

Let us now revisit John 8:44 where Jesus is explaining to the Pharisees and Sadducees and other Jews the differences between Abraham's seed of faith and the seed of the devil. He said to them, letting them know in no uncertain terms that they were the seed of the devil and not of the God of Abraham, "You are of your father the devil, and the desires of your father you want to do. He was a murderer from the beginning, and does not stand in the truth, because there is no truth in him. When he speaks a lie, he speaks from his own resources, for he is a liar and the father of it." And now, let's revisit Mark 8:33 – But when He had turned around and looked at His disciples, He rebuked Peter, saying, "Get behind Me

Satan! For you are not mindful of the things of God, but the things of men." The minds of "men" are the same as the mind of Satan, because they think the thoughts the devil interjects into the minds of his own children. This is vital! The thoughts of the devil and the thoughts of the unredeemed world are the same thoughts for the thoughts of the world originate from the devil! The men of the world that have not received deliverance from mindsets and strongholds nor had become new creatures through our Lord Jesus Christ. Because of that, Jesus was speaking to the devil directly and to the mind of men indirectly at the same time, because they are one and the same. Wow!

In looking at the Babylon in Revelation, I believe that Babylon is used to describe all self-centered governments, businesses, and religions on the face of the earth who are under the influence of the god of this world, and that Mystery Babylon is the symbolic city that unregenerate man builds as he has done since the beginning starting with Cain, the first offspring to sin against God back in the beginning and was sent away to be a vagabond. Genesis 4:16-17 – Then Cain went out from the presence of the LORD and dwelt in the land of Nod on the east of Eden. And Cain knew his wife, and she conceived and bore Enoch. And he built a city, and called the name of the city after the name of his son — Enoch. Notice "out from the presence of the LORD", for that is key. From Cain we move to Nimrod who built the city and tower of Babel. These show unregenerate man, men under the influence of the god of this age, the devil, desiring to build cities for themselves, both before and after the flood, that independent sovereignty system and the desire to control wealth, power, and the expansion of their land. And it seems they were never satisfied. We see it in King Nebuchadnezzar's Babylon and throughout the rest of the Scriptures. Kings were always trying to gain more land or territory. Even today, we see Russia wanting to expand its boundaries, thereby invading Ukraine. And China wanting to take Taiwan as its territory as well as North Korea wanting to take over South Korea.

We also see that the Bible records that the Gentile nations, under the influence of the god of this world, heavily influenced the

Israelites to succumb to their independent sovereignty system especially in the books of Kings after they wanted a king over them like the other nations, for example. And what did God say to their first prophet, Samuel, who had been their God appointed judge? It isn't you they have rejected, it is Me. The people wanted independent sovereignty. We shouldn't think that the influence of the ways of the world was only in the religious arena either, for the political arena was integrated with religion through priests and kings. Also, world historians record priest-kings in Egypt, Greece, and Rome, as well. But God's intent was always to dwell with men by His ways and not for man to build their own type of an independent sovereignty system to please Him and honor themselves. Again, we see that the devil's strategy had not changed. Acts 17:24-25 says "God who made the world and everything in it, since He is Lord of heaven and earth does not dwell in temples made with hands. Nor is He worshipped with men's hands, as though He needed anything, since He gives to all life, breath, and all things."

As I reflected on all the things the Holy Spirit revealed and led me to write about in this book, I realized we went from the extreme mindset of everything is the cause of demons to the extreme mindset of demons aren't interested in us as individuals and therefore not involved in our lives at all. I actually believe that both of those polar viewpoints are also schemes of the enemy to lure us into believing lies and building up mindsets to progress into strongholds if not checked with the Scriptures. I believe the greatest mistake anyone can make is to over or under estimate the influence of the enemy. We must know that his influence doesn't have ultimate power, Jesus does, but it isn't powerless. The influence of the devil is active through his children and the ways of the world. We must be diligent in checking ourselves to see who the influencers over our minds and therefore, our lives are, and if they aren't people of God led by the Holy Spirit, then we need to repent and set our minds in the opposite direction and allow Jesus to lead us into victory with Him as we overcome in Him.

Also, as I was considering all of the things that the Holy Spirit showed me, I came to realize the Bible doesn't really go into a whole lot of detail about the origins of demons, evil and unclean spirits, or the devil's angels, other than God created them and they are tools He manages and uses as He moves and works in the midst of the affairs of men with very distinct good God purposes. These unclean spirits are not allowed to run willy nilly all over the earth to do whatever evil they want or will to do. They are only permitted to do the will of God. God always gives them permission to work with instructions of what they can and cannot do so that they aid Him in His ultimate good plans for us. Yes, they do indeed want to wreak havoc, inflict pain of many kinds, steal from mankind, destroy mankind, and kill mankind because they are undeniably evil and riddled with anger and hatred. But as they operate in that evil and hatred, they are unwittingly doing God's work and driving and compelling men to run into the loving, merciful, and compassionate hands of God as He wills, or if people won't, those people become object learning lessons for others to learn from like the people of Noah's time, the inhabitants of Sodom and Gomorrah, King Saul, Judas, the Pharisees and Sadducees, and Ananias and Saphira, as examples. These object learning lessons then, in turn, cause many to run into the loving, merciful, and compassionate hands of God through His Son, Jesus! Praise His holy name!!

God created many unclean spirits because the devil, or Satan, just is not powerful enough to do all that God knows needs to be done. He's just too small. God is present everywhere, not the devil, God is all knowing, not the devil, God is all powerful, not the devil. The devil is just not "all that" contrary to what some have taught in error, from doctrines of demons, and misguided writers of literature. The most important thing we learn, is that God actually created Satan and his evil angels for the betterment of mankind, for the good of all men. You may be asking, good? What good? Colossians 1:13-18 teaches us – He has delivered us from the power of darkness and conveyed us into the kingdom of the Son of His love, in whom we have redemption through His blood, the forgiveness of sins. He is the image of the invisible God, the firstborn over all creation. For by Him **all things** were created (emphasis mine) that are in heaven and that are on earth, visible and invisible, whether thrones or dominions or principalities or powers. All things were created through Him and "for" Him. And He is before all things, and in Him all things consist. And He is the head of the body, the church, who is the beginning, the firstborn from the dead, that in all things He may have the preeminence. – In answer to the question, that, that right there. That good! See, what the enemy means for evil, God turns around for our good just like in the life of Joseph. He works everything out to the good for those of us who are called according to His purposes, if we allow Him. We need only to choose to run into the loving, compassionate, merciful, hands of God through the loving, compassionate, merciful hands of His only begotten and beloved Son, Jesus, full of grace!

Because of this, as God brings us into maturity, we, the body of Christ, have got to change our mindset on how we view the work of the enemy. It perhaps is the biggest mindset that needs to be changed. We need to shift our thinking from the mindset of fear and/or intimidation when we see the enemy at work, when we recognize the spirit of the world, the spirit of the age, powers, principalities, wickedness in high places, the wiles of the devil, the demonic, etc. to the mindset of seeing God at work here in the midst of it all. We should be seeing God getting ready to move in a mighty way, seeing God baring His Holy arm, setting things right, or see God rolling up His sleeves as it is referred to in the Message version of Psalm 98:1 – He rolled up His sleeves, He set things right. And in Isaiah 52:10 – God has rolled up His sleeves. All the nations can see His Holy muscled arm. We should view it as God moving and working "good" as we see Him using one of His tools from His toolbox. And then we need to set our minds to seek Him as to what He is doing and seek what He would have our part to be within it. We should not be intimidated when we recognize the enemy working, but rather be bold and courageous as the Bible states many times. As a matter of fact, rejoicing when we see the enemy at work because we then know that God is at work and His working is a sure path, route, highway to become matured, encouraged, and emboldened! And of course, beyond bringing in a great harvest of souls, that He is setting the scene for the final battle where we know that the Bride of Christ wins, and triumphs and overcomes through and with Him. Where the city of God defeats the city of unregenerate man, where Father God's kingdom continues throughout all eternity but the kingdom of men of the world with the enemy as their father, collapses and dies forever as Revelation shows us!

What is so exciting to me right now, is that the Lord revealed to me that after He brought the disciples through their process of maturing that we discussed earlier, and once the correct mindsets were built up within them with their brains functioning the way God created them to, as we learned in chapter nine, that is when they were able to move, by the Holy Spirit, into the miraculous. And it is the exact goal He has now for us, His true church, we, the members in particular! Therefore, let us rejoice in this new season He has brought upon the earth and allow Him to lead us not into temptation, but deliver us from evil! Hallelujah!

Thank you, Father, for Jesus, the children's bread, that is our deliverance from not only mindsets and strongholds, but from all things contrary to You and Your plans over us! And may we, as 1 Thessalonians 5:16-23 says – Rejoice always, pray without ceasing, in everything give thanks; for this is the will of God in Christ Jesus for you. Do not quench the Spirit. Do not despise prophesies. Test all things; hold fast what is good. Abstain from every form of evil. Now may the God of peace Himself sanctify you completely; and may your whole spirit, soul, and body be preserved blameless at the coming of our Lord Jesus Christ. Amen!

Other titles from Higher Ground Books & Media:

Forgiven and Not Forgotten by Terra Kern

The Deception of 666 by Terra Kern

Journey to the Mountaintop by Terra Kern

Oasis or Mirage by Terra Kern

Little Jenna Jafferty Series by Terra Kern

Don't Be Stupid (And I Mean That in the Nicest Way) by Rebecca Benston

Full Gospel by Rev. Jerry C. Crossley

Music and the Holy Spirit by Stephen Shepherd

One Day in May by Joanne Piccari Coleman

Soul Solutions by Terri Kozlowski

Man Made by Grace by Willie Deeanjlo White

The Real Prison Diaries by Judy Frisby

The Bottom of This by Tramaine Hannah

The Words of My Father by Mark Tedesco

Add these titles to your collection today!

http://www.highergroundbooksandmedia.com

HIGHER GROUND BOOKS & MEDIA IS AN INDEPENDENT PUBLISHER

Do you have a story to tell?

Higher Ground Books & Media is an independent Christian-based publisher specializing in stories of triumph! Our purpose is to empower, inspire, and educate through the sharing of personal experiences. We are always looking for great, new stories to add to our collection. If you're looking for a publisher, get in touch with us today!

Please be sure to visit our website for our submission guidelines.

http://www.highergroundbooksandmedia.com/submission-guidelines

HGBM SERVICES IS OUR CONSULTING FIRM

AUTHOR SERVICES

HGBM Services offers a variety of writing and coaching services for aspiring authors! We can help with editing, manuscript critiques, self-publishing, and much more! Get in touch today to see how we can help you make your dream of becoming an author a reality!

*****

We also offer social media marketing services for authors, small businesses, and non-profit organizations. Let us help you get the word out about your book, your projects, and your mission. We offer great rates, quality promos, consistent communication, and a personal touch!

http://www.highergroundbooksandmedia.com/editing-writing-services

Need Bulk Copies?

If you would like to order bulk copies of this book or any other title at Higher Ground Books & Media, please contact us at highergroundbooksandmedia@gmail.com.

We offer discounts for purchases of 20 or more copies. Excellent for small groups, book clubs, classrooms, etc.

Get in touch today and get a set of great stories for your students or group members.